a ten week journey
through the book of

JOHN

delight ministries

Delight Ministries
www.delightministries.com

Printed in the United States of America
First Printing: January 2020
Believers Press
ISBN: 978-0-9906825-9-2

OUR MISSION

Our mission is to invite college women into Christ-centered community that fosters vulnerability and transforms stories.

WHO WE ARE

We are a college women's community that grows together, serves together, learns together, and does life together while chasing the heart of God.

WHAT WE DO

We provide college women with the tools and resources to launch, grow, and sustain Christ-centered communities on college campuses. We create curriculum that tells the real stories of college women chasing the heart of God.

TABLE OF CONTENTS

INTRO
mackenzie wilson

Jesus.

Who is He?

So many of us have been around this Jesus guy for *s o o o o* long that if we're being honest, we've lost a bit of the wonder of who He really is.

Others of us just met this guy a few weeks, months, or years ago, and we're not totally sure about all of the details of His life, where He came from, or His whole story.

Then, there are those of us that have so many false ideas of who He is and what He's about that we've started to run in the other direction. These narratives have been shaped by the way we grew up, the pain we've walked through, or the experiences that have fogged our view of this man who is supposedly a savior and a friend.

I'm not sure where you find yourself on the spectrum, but I can promise you that I've been there too. At some point in my life, all of the above statements have rung true. I've purposely held Jesus at arm's length, I've gotten up-close and personal with Him, and I've slowly drifted away without even noticing.

My journey with Jesus has been just that—a journey. A journey that has withstood every question, every doubt, every insecurity, every heartbreak, and every trial. A journey that hasn't come back void, but has consistently shown me that *He is so worth it and He really is that good.*

I am so excited about this journey that we are getting ready to take together. Over the next few months, we will be diving headfirst into the book of John, the fourth gospel. We're going to get to know Jesus in a new way together. We're going to ask questions, put Him to the test, and see if who He says He is rings true. Like doubting Thomas, (Don't know Thomas? No worries, we'll meet him later!) we're going to feel the scars on His hands, get up-close and personal to the story, and see for ourselves just how real He really is.

So, wherever you are on your journey with Jesus, I invite you to use this book as a reintroduction. Let the story wash over you in a new way, look for things you've never seen before, and get to know Him in a fresh way. I promise it will be so worth it! I can't wait to see how we grow, what we learn, and who we become as we step into this life-changing story together.

WHO IS JESUS TO YOU?
the before...

Just write what comes into your mind. What do you know about Jesus today? How have you experienced Him? What confuses you about Him? What doubts or questions do you have about Him?

This doesn't have to be pretty or sound like a sermon. Don't write what you think you're supposed to write. Just write what's in your heart, who you know Him to be, and how He has shown up in your life thus far.

_____

_____

_____

_____

_____

_____

_____

_____

_____

_____

_____

_____

_____

_____

_____

_____

_____

_____

_____

TIPS FOR READING SCRIPTURE

The truth is, reading Scripture isn't always easy! It's a muscle that you have to stretch and grow over time. We've compiled a list of tips from the Delight team that we think will help you to start to love your daily time in the Word. These are all practical tips that will help you to better hear the voice of God through Scripture.

1. Prepare Your Heart – This is SO simple! Every day before you open the Word, ask God to simply prepare your heart, show up, and speak to you. Reading the Bible isn't something we have to do on our own or through our own power. The Word is alive—meaning that God can and will speak to you through it. All you have to do is ask!

2. Ask Good Questions – This can seriously change the way you encounter the Bible! The best tool we have to understand the Word of God is our own ability to ask the right questions. If you've ever read Scripture and not understood something (*a.k.a. me every day of my life...*) that's an invitation to ask a question. *What? When? How? Where? Who? Why?* Dig into your questions and seek out answers!

For some of your more historical or practical questions, you can read biblical commentaries, get a study Bible, or talk to someone who knows more than you. For the other more complex questions, bring them to the feet of Jesus and simply ask. He cares and can provide answers in some of the coolest ways! This isn't your college calculus class where you have to be afraid to ask in the fear of looking stupid. There is a loving, caring, and gentle Father on the other end of the line ready to dialogue with you.

If this is new to you…don't worry! We're going to ask A LOT of questions of the text together in this book.

3. Read at Your Own Pace – Take your time with reading Scripture! You have your entire life to read the Bible. If you want to meditate on one verse for an entire week—do it! If you want to read the entire Bible in a month—do that too! Go at the pace that feels comfortable to you. Don't be afraid to slow down and dive really deep in certain parts when you feel led to.

#4 Talk About What You're Learning – Some of the best moments of revelation from Scripture happen by simply talking to the people around you about the things you've been reading. This isn't a journey you have to make alone! Be sure to talk about how God is speaking to you through His Word with your roommate, friends, parents, and your Delight community!

#5 Follow the Spirit – When you're reading your Bible, don't be afraid to change course from where you initially started. You may start out reading John, but then feel a nudge to re-read that Psalm you heard the other day. Don't ignore those nudges! When you open up your heart to hear from the Lord, He may redirect you to another passage of Scripture and that is absolutely okay. You never know what He might be leading you to.

INTRO TO JOHN

Before we jump into the first chapter of John, I want to give you a little bit more about the context and background of this book.

In order to really understand John, you have to understand how John fits in with the rest of the gospel testimonies.

To put it bluntly, the book of John is kind of like the red-headed step child. It definitely stands out! Matthew, Mark, and Luke are actually referred to as the Synoptic Gospels because they are so similar. They tell the same stories, follow a similar sequence of events, and even use some of the same retelling and wording. **John on the other hand did things with his own flair and style!**

Here's a breakdown of the four Gospels, their intended audiences, and their unique traits:

Matthew – Matthew was a Jewish follower of Jesus who was writing to his fellow Jews. He wanted to convince them that Jesus was the Messiah and King for whom they had been waiting. That's why he talks about so many of the prophecies from the Old Testament that were fulfilled through Jesus.

Mark – Mark wrote to tell the Romans about Jesus. It's the shortest gospel, doesn't have much fluff, and focuses more on the deeds of Christ. For Mark, the proof was in the pudding! He showed us how awesome Jesus was rather than simply telling us!

Luke – Luke wrote to tell the Gentiles, basically anybody who wasn't Jewish, about Jesus. His book is very detail-oriented (check chapter 1 for a complete genealogy of Jesus all the way back to Adam!). He talks about the humanity of Jesus and His connection to all people, not just Jews.

John – John was writing for everyone (Jew, Gentile, Roman, Greek, etc.). He is our most artistic and creative gospel writer. His goal was to convince people to believe in Jesus as the Son of God and he does it in an incredibly beautiful way. The word **believe** is actually found one hundred times in the book of John. In John 20:30-31 he even comes out and gives us his purpose for writing—point blank:

"Jesus performed many other signs in the presence of his disciples, which are not recorded in this book. But these are written that you may believe that Jesus is the Messiah, the Son of God, and that by believing you may have life in his name."

While Matthew, Mark, and Luke focus primarily on what Jesus did, John places a heavier emphasis on who Jesus is—the Son of God. He does this by telling us about seven signs or miracles that Jesus performed (six of these miracles aren't mentioned in the other Gospels), highlighting seven "I am" statements (not included in the other Gospels), and by introducing us to eyewitness testimonies which speak to the identity of Jesus.

7 "I AM" STATEMENTS OF JESUS

the bread of life
john 6:35, 41, 48, 51

the light of the world
john 8:12

the gate of the sheep
john 10:7, 9

**the resurrection
and the life**
john 11:25

the good shepherd
john 10:11, 14

**the way, the truth,
and the life**
john 14:6

the true vine
john 15:1, 5

7 MIRACLES OF JESUS

water into wine
john 2:1-11

healing the official's son
john 4:43-54

healing at the pool of bethesda
john 5:1-9

the feeding of the 5000
john 6:1-5

walking on the water
john 6:16-25

healing the man born blind
john 9:1-41

raising lazarus from the dead
john 11:1-44

HOW THIS BOOK WORKS

SCRIPTURE: Each week you'll be reading anywhere from one to four chapters in John. The chapters in this book will walk you through the reading process. As you read, you'll answer questions, fill in blanks, and hopefully get a deeper understanding of the context behind what you're reading. You'll want to pull out your Bible and start reading any time you see something like this....

Go and read John 22.

Just remember that gray highlights are your cue to pause and open the Word. Each week, we will zero in on one topic that the Scripture text introduces. Our prayer is that this book brings new light to Bible stories and verses that you've perhaps read a million times.

STORY: Each week you'll read the story of a REAL college girl or recent graduate. She will share how she has seen that week's Scripture text at work in her life. Our prayer is that you see yourself in the midst of each and every one of the stories and that you're able to begin to identify how God might be present in your story too.

CONVERSATION STARTERS: Our goal is to get the conversation rolling between you and the Lord, as well as within your Delight community. These 4-6 questions will help you do just that for every week! We suggest setting some time aside each week to answer these questions in a prayerful way with the Lord. Then, come ready to discuss them with your Delight community. The more time you take to prepare on the front end—the better your conversations will be!

DELIGHT DATE IDEAS: Delight dates are your opportunity to meet one-on-one with someone from the Delight community. You can use the ideas and prompts for each week to give you an idea of how to spend your time together. We hope that you find some amazing new friends through this weekly practice.

WHEN HE CALLS YOU

John 1

Here we are! It's Week 1 and we're ready to step into our first passage of Scripture from John. We want to start off slow, so this week we're only covering one chapter—the first chapter of John. But trust us...there is a LOT packed into this week—51 verses to be exact!

Are you feeling overwhelmed? Don't worry! We're doing this together, every step of the way!

John 1 covers a lot of ground, and we could go into detail on every verse but this week we want to zero in on the **calling of the disciples** and sit with the **calling that Jesus has placed on our lives too.**

The book of John starts off unlike the rest of the Gospels. Instead of diving into the details of the life of Jesus, John leads off with a poem that sets the tone for his writing:

In the beginning was the Word, and the Word was with God, and the Word was God. He was with God in the beginning. Through him all things were made;

without him nothing was made that has been made.
In him was life, and that life was the light of all
mankind. The light shines in the darkness, and the
darkness has not overcome it.

John 1:1-5

This is so much more than a pretty introduction—this is the point of the whole book, wrapped up in a couple profound sentences, setting the stage for the story of Jesus. Think of this as the preview or the trailer for what we're getting ready to encounter in Him.

Fill in the blanks below from John 1:1.

In the beginning was _____,
and _____ *was with God,*
and _____ *was God.*

At first glance, this can come off as a little confusing! I mean, *hello*, I thought we were talking about Jesus... so what is "the Word?"

In order to understand what this means we have to know the translation of "the Word" in Greek. It's **Logos.**

The idea of *Logos* has deep and rich roots in both Jewish and Greek thinking. Ancient Jews often used *Logos* and the word for God interchangeably. They believed that "Word of God" could be used to perfectly represent God Himself. On the other hand, Greek philosophers used *Logos* to describe the power that made sense out of the chaos of the world. *Logos* was essentially the "Supreme Reason" that controlled all things.

So here, John is leading off his book about Jesus by speaking the language of both the Jews and Greeks. (Remember the book of John is for everyone!) He's essentially saying, "For centuries you've been talking and writing about the Word (*Logos*). Now I'm going to explain to you who the Word is."

Spoiler alert—it's Jesus! Now let's go back and fill in verse 1 again with this new information. Replace "the Word" with "Jesus."

In the beginning was _____,

and _____ *was with God,*

and _____ *was God.*

Jesus has always been a part of God's greater story. At the creation of the world, He was there. In the garden of Eden, He was there. When the Israelites crossed the Red Sea, He was there. With King David on the battlefield, He was there. During the exile and the return of the Israelite people, He was there. Jesus has always been wherever "there" is, and John is getting ready to introduce us to the fullness of His character and being.

You see, Jesus IS God—He's not God Junior, God's sidekick, or God's assistant. He's the fullness of God Himself. But while Jesus is God, Jesus is *not* the Father. I know this sounds a little tricky, but this is our understanding of the Holy Trinity (Father, Son, Holy Spirit). They are all equally God, yet they are distinct to themselves. The Father is not the Son. The Son is not the Father. The Spirit is not Jesus. They are all distinct, yet they are all one God in three persons. We're going to dive deeper into this concept throughout the book of John! So no worries if you're still a little confused.

+ In verse six, John switches things up and introduces us to the first eyewitness who will testify about the identity of Jesus. What's his name? (v. 6)

SIDE NOTE: *This isn't the author of the book; this is a different John—known as John the Baptist. We're going to learn a lot more about him in a bit, but for now, know that John the Baptist was focused on bringing people to faith in the Messiah, Jesus. John the Baptist knew that he wasn't the light, but was sent to bear witness and to pave the way for the light (a.k.a. Jesus).*

Verse 10 gets into some interesting stuff. Fill in the blanks below.

He was in the _____, *and though the* _____ *was made through him, the* _____ *did not recognize him. He came to that which was his own, but his own did not receive him.*

I love this repetition and how verse 1 mirrors verse 10! Serious props to John for this literary masterpiece.

Verse 10 and 11 introduce this idea that God came to the same world He created, yet the world did not know Him. This is foreshadowing what's to come in the rest of John's story. Greek experts say that a better way to translate "He came to that which was his own" would be, "He came home." Jesus came home and His own family didn't accept Him. The Jewish people, the very people He created and sustained, were the ones who put Him to death on a cross. But there is good news! What's so beautiful about this story is that instead of being marked by mankind's rejection of Jesus—**it's marked by Jesus's acceptance of mankind.** Let's check out verses 12-13.

Yet to all who did receive him, to those who believed in his name, he gave the right to become children of God—children born not of natural descent, nor of human decision or a husband's will, but born of God.

WHOA! That's us! That's *our* invitation into a *personal* relationship with the Word (*Logos*), which we now know means Jesus Christ Himself. **When we believe Jesus is who He says He is, we get to be a part of the family! We become children of God.**

The next part of John 1 gives us a glimpse into the baptism of Jesus through the eyes of John the Baptist (remember him from earlier?). If you want to read more about John the Baptist's backstory, head to Luke 1:5-25 for a full account of his birth. Here are the highlights about John that you need to know: First off, he's related to Jesus...but we're pretty sure they weren't neighborhood pals growing up. They didn't actually meet face-to-face until adulthood, as described through this moment in John 1. Second, John the Baptist is a pretty...*radical* guy. Matthew 3:1-6 gives us some interesting details about his fashion choices and dietary preferences.

+ What were his clothes like? What kind of food did he eat? (Matthew 3:4)

Third, (author) John describes John the Baptist as a witness to Jesus.

One of the coolest parts about Scripture is the thread woven throughout, connecting the Old Testament prophesies with actual events described in the New Testament. Check out John 1:22-23. Now flip to Isaiah 40:3. See the connection?

John the Baptist was sent to prepare the way of the Lord. His baptism pointed people to the coming of King Jesus.

Read John 1:29-34.

Finally... Jesus is officially on the scene. Woot woot!

Now we're going to see Jesus in action as He calls His first followers. You'll notice throughout the rest of John 1 that Jesus called people into *relationship* with Him in very different ways. Jesus met each person where they were and extended a unique invitation to leave everything behind and follow Him. Go ahead and read John 1:35-41.

In verses 35-37 we're introduced to two men who decided to follow Jesus simply because of the testimony of John. Verse 38 describes them lurking around Jesus, and I love His response—He asked a simple question: "What do you want?" At first, this might sound kind of abrupt and off-putting, but think about it...

This is the first recorded question of Jesus in the Gospels. Jesus wanted to know—what did they want in following Him? Did they want something only for themselves? Did they just want an answer to prayer? Did they want fame or attention? Did they want to prove Him wrong? Or did they simply want to *be with Him?*

It's important that we ask ourselves the same question.

What do we want from Jesus? What are we *truly* looking for in following Him?

The two men responded by asking Jesus where He was staying. Maybe that sounds just a tiny bit creepy to us, but I like to think that in those days it was normal to start conversations with, "Hey man! Where do you live?"

I love what happened next! The two men spent the day with Jesus, and then one of them (Andrew, the brother of Simon Peter and one of the 12 disciples) ran to tell his brother. After spending just one day in the presence of Jesus, Andrew was absolutely convinced that he had encountered the One for whom the people of God had been waiting. That's why he ran to tell his brother with total confidence, "We have found the Messiah" (John 1:41).

What in the world did Jesus say or do that day to give Andrew such clarity? Was it the way Jesus talked? Was it the stories that He told? Was it the way He interacted with people? Was it the way He listened or the answers that He gave? Was it a miracle that He performed? *What was it?*

Andrew somehow knew that Jesus was the long-awaited Messiah. All we know is that hanging out with Jesus for one day opened his mind and changed his life forever. I think Andrew's story is (or could be) just like a lot of our own stories. One day, one encounter, one touch with Jesus— changes *everything*.

In verse 42 we're introduced to Simon, who received the new name *Cephas* (translated to Peter) from Jesus. You can read an in-depth account in Luke 5:1-11, but what's important to know is Peter's call to follow Jesus happened through a miraculous encounter—ultimately bringing Peter to the feet of Jesus, where he made the decision to leave everything behind and follow Him.

Let's keep reading! We're at verse 43, where Jesus called His next two disciples. Jesus was hanging out in Galilee when He came across Philip and straight up told Philip to follow Him. Philip goes to find his friend to invite him to come along too. (Aww! What a good friend!)

+ What was that friend's name? (v. 45)

Check out their convo in The Passion Translation:

Then Philip went to look for his friend, Nathanael, and told him, "We've found him! We've found the One we've been waiting for! It's Jesus, son of Joseph from Nazareth, the Anointed One! He's the One that Moses and the prophets prophesied would come!" Nathanael sneered, "Nazareth! What good thing could ever come from Nazareth?" Philip answered, "Come and let's find out!"

John 1:45-46 TPT

Okay, clearly Nathanael was not having it! He was not buying this whole "the One we've been waiting for" thing! Nathanael approached Jesus with a doubting and suspicious heart. I love what happens next. Go ahead and finish reading John 1.

Don't you kind of relate to this? Nathanael was low-key hating on Jesus when Jesus walked up and immediately gave him a compliment. He said, "Here truly is an Israelite in whom there is no deceit."

Jesus was basically declaring that Nathanael was pure-hearted, and there was nothing tricky or deceitful about him (LOL). He then said that He saw Nathanael sitting under a fig tree. Because that knowledge must have been supernatural, Jesus's simple statement fully convinced Nathanael of who Jesus was and how worthy He was of following.

We can only guess what Nathanael was doing under that fig tree, but I like to think that whatever it was deeply mattered to him. Maybe he was praying, maybe he was studying Scripture, or confessing his sins—but the fact that Jesus noticed gave him the full confidence that this was the One he could give his whole heart to.

I love the story of Nathanael because it reminds us that **we're all in need of a Savior.** Every single one of us is looking for someone or something to place our trust in and follow.

Many of us have been following culture, letting it tell us what matters, and believing it has the answer about what we need to do or say to get ahead. Some of us have been following the opinions of other people in our lives, trying to impress them or prove our worth by doing what we think they want. Still others of us are following a "dream" or a path that we've created for ourselves. We're swept up in the lie that once we get *that* job or reach *that* goal, it will all be worth it. You see? We're all following something.

I love that John 1 reminds us that **we've all received the invitation to leave behind whatever has been consuming our life and to simply follow Jesus.** In Jesus there is purpose, hope, love, acceptance, peace, joy, freedom, and so much more.

Check out what Jesus said to Nathanael after he committed to following Jesus (v. 50):

Jesus said, "You believe because I told you I saw you under the fig tree. You will see greater things than that." He then added, "Very truly I tell you, you will see 'heaven open, and the angels of God ascending and descending on' the Son of Man."

Greater things are ahead. **Following Jesus is a decision that unlocks the kingdom of heaven in our lives.** *It's so worth it!*

Trust us...you haven't seen anything yet! I can't wait to jump into more of the book of John with you next week!

my WHEN HE CALLS YOU story

megan miller

Hi! My name is Megan and this is my *"When He Calls You"* story!

I love reading about the moment that Jesus called some of the disciples in John 1. It gets me thinking about the moment when Jesus found me, told me to leave everything behind, and follow Him.

I was a freshman at the University of Oregon following everything but Jesus.

Once I arrived at college, I started looking for the "typical" college experience full of hooking up, smoking weed, attending frat parties, and posting game day pics with beautiful sorority sisters. For the most part, I had accomplished everything I had set out to do my freshman year. I was the QUEEN of the party scene! A typical Friday night for me looked like spending hours attempting to look hot, getting blackout drunk, and ending up in some guy's dorm room for a quick fix hookup.

One night I found myself in my usual routine on my way to a guy's place, planning to sleep over. That's when I heard it...

"You don't have to do this."

I knew who it was immediately. I had grown up around the Christian scene enough to know that a voice in your head could be God trying to talk to you. But I refused to believe that He was real. So I (internally) said back, *"You're not real."*

I repeated it over and over in my head trying to convince myself that I could keep running in the other direction. I continued on my way, hooked up with the guy that night, and woke up feeling just as empty, lost, and lonely as I had every day before that.

One week later I was back home in California where I found myself at a sunrise Easter service, during which a woman shared her testimony about this guy Jesus who had changed everything for her. Her story was *exactly* my story.

I got home that day and cried to my parents, told them everything I had been doing, and sat there unsure of what to do next. The next morning there was a knock at my door—it was the woman who had shared her testimony at the sunrise service. She prayed with me and left me a Daily Bible and a simple invitation: to give Jesus a chance.

So that's what I did. I went back to school, told all my friends I was on a cleanse (I didn't have the guts to tell them I wasn't drinking because of Jesus), started reading my Bible every day, and talked to God. Lo and behold, everything started to change! Here I am now, six years later, confident that my decision to give Jesus a try was the best decision I've ever made.

Sometimes I think back on my story and wish that my "come to Jesus" moment looked a little more like Andrew's. I wish that all it took was one look at Jesus to convince me—but honestly, I think I'm a little more like Nathanael. I was quite literally running in the other direction, sneering at the voice of God. But my *"When He Calls You"* story truly has nothing to do with my rejection of Him and everything to do with His acceptance of me.

You see, it doesn't matter if your story is like Andrew's, or Peter's, or Nathanael's, or anyone else for that matter. It doesn't matter how you got there, all that matters is that you receive the acceptance you already have in Him, and choose to put your hope and trust in who He is.

There wasn't anything special about the disciples, the first people Jesus called. They were ordinary people with ordinary problems a lot like you and me. But what changed the trajectory of their lives was their simple decision to follow Jesus. You have that same invitation today and every day! We don't have to be ashamed of how we got here— we can joyfully look forward to all that lies ahead on this journey with Jesus.

CONVERSATION STARTERS

+ What did you learn about Jesus's character in John 1? It can be something new that you realized or something you were reminded of.

_____

_____

_____

_____

_____

_____

_____

_____

_____

+ Which one of the disciple's stories is most reminiscent of your own testimony?

> + **Andrew:** *You had one day, one touch, or one encounter with Jesus and you knew you had to follow Him.*
> + **Simon Peter:** *It took a little more convincing for you! You needed to witness His power through a life change or a miracle in order to surrender at His feet.*
> + **Nathanael:** *You doubted Him at first and held Him at arm's length before deciding to follow Him.*
> + *You're not sure if you're fully following Jesus yet, but you're excited to continue on this journey!*

_____

_____

_____

_____

+ What is one thing that you've been "following" other than Jesus.

_____

_____

_____

_____

_____

_____

_____

_____

_____

+ We love the question that Jesus asked Andrew and his friend when they began to follow Him: "What do you want?" What are you specifically looking for in a commitment to follow Jesus?

_____

_____

_____

_____

_____

_____

_____

_____

_____

+ So many of the disciples were led to Jesus because of the testimony of someone else. With whom specifically can you simply share your story this week?

_____

_____

_____

_____

DELIGHT DATE IDEA

Share with your Delight date your own *"When He Calls You"* story! Was there a moment that changed everything for you? How did Jesus pursue your heart and how did you respond? Take note of how your stories are similar and how they differ!

MY DELIGHT DATE'S NAME: _____

DATE/TIME/PLACE: _____
_____

HOW I CAN BE PRAYING FOR MY DELIGHT DATE:
_____
_____
_____
_____

OTHER NOTES: _____
_____
_____
_____
_____
_____
_____
_____
_____
_____
_____

in the
beginning was
THE WORD
and the
word was
WITH GOD
and the word
WAS GOD.

john 1:1

WHEN HE MAKES YOU NEW

John 2-4

This week, we're continuing our journey through the book of John, covering John chapters 2-4. We're speeding things up a bit because we have a lot of ground to cover! What's cool about these three chapters is how they're connected by a common theme. John is going to introduce us to the good news that Jesus is in the business of making **all things new.**

We will see this theme start to take shape through these moments...

+ Water replaced by **new wine** at a wedding in Cana
+ Jesus foretelling the rebuilding of Himself as the **new temple**
+ The **new birth** Jesus speaks of to a curious Pharisee named Nicodemus
+ The **new water and worship** that transforms the life of a controversial woman in Samaria

We will see it over and over again—**old being made new**. My prayer is that as we study Scripture together this week, you begin recognizing how Jesus is at work in your life bringing what was once old and lifeless into a new beginning.

Grab your Bible and turn to John 2. <mark>Go ahead and read verses 1-12.</mark>

On the third day a wedding took place at Cana in Galilee. Jesus's mother was there, and Jesus and his disciples had also been invited to the wedding.

John 2:1-2

Three days after Jesus called Nathanael to follow Him, Jesus, the disciples, and Jesus's mother all attended a wedding in the city of Cana. We can guess that because they were all in attendance, this was probably a major community event. Everybody in Cana had probably been talking about this wedding!

SIDE NOTE: *It's pretty wild to think that Jesus and His disciples were sometimes just normal guys who attended weddings like you and me! Some of us maybe wouldn't have thought of Jesus as the party-going type, but His presence at a wedding party actually gives us a glimpse into His heart.*

+ Mary approached her son Jesus and let Him in on a problem. What was the problem? (v. 3)

The party was going along smoothly until suddenly the wine ran out. So what? Party's over! No biggie! Maybe it doesn't seem like a big deal to us, but we can see the gravity of this problem if we explore the context of weddings in Jewish culture. Weddings during the time of Jesus were a BIG deal. They were lengthy celebrations that could last up to a week. Unlike in our culture today, the groom's family typically was responsible for planning and financing the wedding celebration, of which wine was a crucial part. Keep in mind that the wine during biblical times wasn't like our wine today—it was diluted with water to about one-third of the strength of your average bottle from the grocery store. Drinking wine was more like drinking water (so Jesus wasn't trying to get lit). You can think of running out of wine at a wedding equivalent with showing up to a coffee shop for your morning cup of joe only to be told they've run out. It was a BIG DEAL! In the Jewish custom, this would've brought a lot of embarrassment and disgrace upon the groom and his family in terms of social standing.

What happened next is super interesting. Jesus responded to His mother, "Woman, why do you involve me? My hour has not yet come" (v. 4).

Is Jesus rebuking her? Is He objecting? Is He being rude? Like…what is going on?

To us, Jesus's response might sound harsh, but Jesus wasn't being hostile toward His mom. The word we translate to "woman" was actually a term used to show respect in biblical times. However, by not referring to her as His family, Jesus marked a transition in His relationship with her—He moved from being her Son to being her Savior. This is a subtle way of noting that things are about to change… and *wow do things change!*

Nearby stood six stone water jars, the kind used by the Jews for ceremonial washing, each holding from twenty to thirty gallons.

John 2:6

+ What does John say the water jars were used for? (v. 6)

Verse 6 tells us that there were six stone water jars for Jewish purification. The water held in these containers was likely used for washing the hands and feet of the guests as well as the dishes for the party.

Let's note: it's by no accident that John is referencing the water jar's connection to the old order of Jewish law and custom. **Jesus is getting ready to replace the old with something better.**

Jesus told the servants to fill the jars to the brim and then take some to the master of the banquet. (Think of this as like the head waiter or party planner.)

I love that the first miracle of Jesus was a secret only revealed to the servants! The party attendees experienced the miracle, but the servants experienced the miracle maker. The least noticed people in the room by culture's standards were the people that Jesus decided to use for the miraculous transformation of water to wine. It's not just cool, it's revealing of His heart!

According to verse 9, after taking a sip, the party's master was stunned at this new wine, and had no idea where it came from. He was so impressed that the bridegroom had saved the best wine for last when most people would've served their best wine first. *The best wine was saved for last!* Isn't that true in the Kingdom? For those of us that are walking with Jesus here on Earth, the best is always yet to come!

And just like that—water was transformed into wine and the **PROBLEM was SOLVED!**

You might be asking yourself why Jesus chose to turn water to wine in secret as His first miracle. Why didn't He do something more important or groundbreaking? Why didn't He do something more public or noticeable? Why did He simply save a party when He could do so much more?

The quiet miracle of Jesus turning water into wine had so much significance for what was about to come for the Jewish people. A nation of people who had been walking in darkness for years, clinging to their old ways, was about to meet the Light that would bring them into a new day and a new dawn.

Old becoming new. Darkness to light. Death to life.

Jesus is doing the same in our lives today. He's calling us to let go of what we've always known, to let go of what feels safe and comfortable, and to step into the newness that only He can offer.

Jesus is doing a new thing.

Many of us have focused our sight so much on the past that we're blinded to the new and good things that God is trying to do in our lives. Maybe there's a past relationship that you don't want to lose, an old dream that you're trying to fit into a new calling from the Lord, or perhaps it's an old sin that you just can't seem to shake.

I want you to stop for a moment and hear Jesus sweetly calling you to let go of the old and to embrace the new, even if it feels scary and unfamiliar. In the kingdom of God, the best wine, the best gifts, and the best blessings that Jesus has to offer always lie ahead of us. It's time to let go of the old and step completely into newness with Him.

As you finish out this week, take your time reading through

the rest of John 2-4 as you take note of Jesus making all things new. Use the outline below to follow along as you read. Ask the Lord to start showing you specific places in your own life where you're still clinging to your old habits, patterns, and ways. Pray that His spirit would loosen the shackles of the old and set you free to step into the new.

SCRIPTURE	John 2:13-23	John 3:1-21	John 4:1-42
SETTING	The temple courtyard in Jerusalem	Jerusalem at night	The town of Sychar in Samaria
MAIN CHARACTERS	Jewish leaders & Jesus	Nicodemus & Jesus	Woman at the well & Jesus
OLD WAY	The physical temple was the place for Jewish worship and the literal home of God's Spirit or presence in Jerusalem.	In verse 4, Nicodemus references the Jewish assumption that his racial identity or birthright assured him a place in God's Kingdom.	The Samaritan woman speaks of water for drinking, like water from the well of Jacob. The Samaritan woman refers to the validity of the Jewish custom that worship had to happen in Jerusalem.
NEW WAY	In verse 18, Jesus refers to His death and resurrection. Through the resurrection, all people would have access to worship God in Spirit and in Truth, not just in the temple in Jerusalem.	Jesus speaks of a new birth or the opportunity for all to be "reborn" through water and Spirit.	Jesus speaks of "living water" that will eternally quench spiritual thirst. Jesus speaks of the time to come when all would be invited to worship in Spirit and in truth.

my WHEN HE MAKES YOU NEW story
makayla white

Hi! My name is Makayla, and this is my *"When He Makes You New"* story!

When I think about Jesus making all things new, some interesting things come to mind: my fear of change, the difficulty of going from the known to the unknown, and how in order to make something new—the old has to be exposed.

Growing up as a Christian girl in the southern United States has its pros and cons. On the pros list: hearing the gospel, knowing the Bible, and being part of a community that knows Jesus. From before I was even born, the norm had been established—attendance at church any time the doors were open, and an emphasis on God in *every* aspect of life. Although this was routine for me as I grew up, I would now describe this as cultural Christianity, a *head* knowledge but not a *heart* knowledge. This system puts a huge emphasis on rule-following, and "because I said so" was my understanding of how to be a Christ-follower. In this cultural faith, so much of the truth of the gospel moving us from death to life is lost—if you can just "fake it till you make it" then you can get by on routine and appearance rather than cultivating a deep and meaningful relationship with God.

And if appearance is what truly matters, then there's a really big opportunity for secret, hidden sin to take root. By the time I reached college, I lived a full-on double life, clinging to a delusion that I was a "good Christian girl" as long as no one knew any different and I could maintain the image.

I basically hid all my darkness within the messages on my phone or in the back seat of a car. I developed patterns where I only felt confident if I had a few guys that I was in text-only relationships with, where we talked a lot about "what we would do if we were together" and sending the pictures they asked for in order to keep them interested. Or I lied to myself about a "good guy" who was just a "friend with benefits"—that as long as no one else knew, I could compartmentalize it so well that it wouldn't have any effect on me.

No one in my college environment truly knew me, so I could fake the Christian persona really easily. I jumped into college ministries, attended Bible studies, and built Christ-centered community, all while keeping a lot hidden and withholding my true self for the sake of upholding a very cultivated façade. I began to idolize virginity, basically believing that as long as I didn't have sex, then everything I was hiding wasn't *really* a big deal, wasn't *really* hurting me, and God didn't *really* care. I definitely was not seeking any of the "new and better" that God had come to give me—rather, I settled for the "old and fake." If we are talking the water to wine story, I had pretty much said, "No thanks, no new and better wine for me, I'll drink the dish water."

When the idol of the title "virgin" came crashing down at the beginning of senior year, my two lives collided. The dark, hidden basement of my life was flooded by the head knowledge I touted, the Jesus I "knew" but didn't let know me, and the gospel of Light. I felt God meet me at rock bottom and tell me He loved me too much to leave me there. I felt half of me had been asleep and was waking up to a brand-new day.

At first, I was totally frozen, overwhelmed...I had a lot of fear about leaving the known for the unknown, living in freedom and light. With every guy I cut loose, I felt some anxiety as the enemy whispered insecurities to me. I didn't know how to talk to God about this and for a while my prayer was for the right words to come. But God was working in my life! He was pursuing me so intentionally and poured so much mercy and grace over me that eventually I was able to tell some trusted friends my WHOLE story. I spilled my guts, I felt so exposed—but *every single one* of them responded with love and encouragement. There were no words of condemnation but instead words of hope that a **new and better** way of living was God's promise!

I truly felt myself moving from old to new—from darkness to light. I can remember being at a candlelight Christmas Eve service, where at the end everyone blows out their candles and the lights come on. I remember thinking that was how my life felt; for so many years I had only let the light in my life be as bright as a candle so the darkness would stay hidden. But now a switch had flipped and the room was flooded with real light. It hurt my eyes at first, but when they adjusted, I could finally see what life was really meant to look like.

Through a conversation with one of my closest friends, I realized the root of the problem: I had convinced myself that I wasn't worthy of being made new. I believed that I had to grab onto what I could because I wasn't worthy of the absolute best God had for me. **Embracing my worth in Christ and receiving not just the new, but also the BETTER, is the journey I'm still on today.** Believing every day that God never gives a poor portion to His children but instead lavishes us with new and better. Working with God to build a true relationship with Him, extending an invitation for Him to work in every aspect of my life. In a way, I feel as if God has built a **new temple** out of me, a place where He dwells rather than a place I hide from Him.

In every story—wine to water, new birth, new temple, new water and worship—all that was old, dark, and sinful was brought out into the open and acknowledged by Jesus. He let everyone know that He wasn't blind to the mess. With us, He sees the old, knows it, and acknowledges that the fullness of His miracle comes from by embracing what is true about Him, knowing His love can radically transform our lives. As the woman at the well shows us, **letting ourselves be made new leads us to a true and better relationship with God, where praise pours out of us without anything to hide.**

CONVERSATION STARTERS

+ What did you learn about Jesus's character in John 2-4? It can be something new that you realized or something you were reminded of.

_____

_____

_____

_____

_____

_____

_____

_____

_____

_____

_____

+ Reflect back on a time in your life when you witnessed Jesus bringing something from old to new. How difficult was it to let go of the "old" in that moment?

_____

_____

_____

_____

_____

_____

_____

_____

_____

_____

+ In the grand scheme of things, Jesus turning water to wine didn't seem all that significant or important. Is there a situation in your life that you've given up on because it seems insignificant or hopeless?

_____

_____

_____

_____

_____

_____

_____

_____

_____

_____

_____

_____

+ Identify a part of your character or spirit which is stuck in old patterns or habits. What would it look like to do the hard work of letting Jesus bring you into a new season in this area?

_____

_____

_____

_____

_____

_____

_____

_____

_____

_____

_____

DELIGHT DATE IDEA

Let's not hold back. Let's not hide anymore. Get real and get truthful. Share with your Delight date the thing in your life that you haven't let Jesus take from old to new. What are you still holding onto because you don't believe Jesus can replace it with something better? Spend some time in prayer with each other asking God to loosen the shackles of the "old" so you can step into the new.

MY DELIGHT DATE'S NAME: _____

DATE/TIME/PLACE: _____
_____

HOW I CAN BE PRAYING FOR MY DELIGHT DATE:
_____
_____
_____
_____

OTHER NOTES: _____
_____
_____
_____
_____
_____
_____
_____
_____
_____

it's time to let go of **THE OLD** and embrace **THE NEW** with Jesus.

WHEN YOU'RE TIRED OF TRYING SO HARD

John 5-6

Welcome back! Today we are continuing our journey through John, reading chapters 5 and 6. Get ready—we're about to see a lot of cool signs and miracles! Let's just say, the word is starting to spread around Judea about this guy who is turning water to wine, healing the sick, and feeding the multitude. Jesus is starting to become a pretty big deal! But not everyone is a fan—a lot of the Jewish leaders are skeptical about who Jesus says He is. We're going to see how Jesus responds to this newfound skepticism, attention, and fame while also getting an inside look at His relationship with His Father in heaven.

Last week we ended with John 4, as Jesus journeyed back to Galilee from Jerusalem. This was after the trip during which Jesus spoke to the woman at the well in Samaria and healed the government official's son as He got back to town. *(Jesus really used those bathroom and snack stops to His full advantage.)*

John 5 picks up with Jesus returning to Jerusalem to observe one of the Jewish holy days, although we don't know which one in particular because John doesn't say.

SIDE NOTE: *The writer John is definitely more type B than type A. He's not exactly great with details. If you're a detail-oriented person, the book of Luke will be your best friend!*

While in Jerusalem, Jesus found Himself at the pools of Bethesda, where many disabled people waited in the hope of finding healing. The commentary *The Gospel According to John* by D.A. Carson mentions a commonly held belief that an angel of the Lord would sometimes come and stir the water, and the first person in the pool would be relieved of their suffering and healed (pg. 242).

Jesus approached one man who had been struggling with an illness for 38 years and asked him simply if he wanted to be healed. He then told him to get up, pick up his mat, and start walking. Just like that, the man was healed! Another miracle moment! This time, there's only one problem...

Remember the Sabbath day by keeping it holy. Six days you shall labor and do all your work, but the seventh day is a sabbath to the LORD your God. On it you shall not do any work, neither you, nor your son or daughter, nor your male or female servant, nor your animals, nor any foreigner residing in your towns.

Exodus 20:8-10

This miracle moment from Jesus happened on the Sabbath—*the Jewish rhythm of abstaining from work and taking time for rest and worship.* Jewish laws were pretty strict when it came to Sabbath. Our modern take on Sabbath is a very watered-down version of what it looked like during biblical times. The Jewish leaders had taken the Law from Exodus 20 and turned it into their obsession. Jesus healing and the man carrying his mat on the Sabbath were direct violations of *their* interpretation of Scripture. The original commandment for God's people to halt their work was so skewed by the added rules and regulations that it was basically impossible to rest. The leaders argued over the true definition of "work" and how they could stay in total right standing with God as the religious elite through their ability to obey the law.

Go read John 5:9-14 to check out their response to the healing.

Sometimes I think about the Pharisees and the Jewish leaders and my first instinct is to turn my nose up at them and their obsession with the Law. It's hard for me to understand how they could miss something so *obvious*. Clearly God was at work in Jesus healing that man. How could they be so consumed with anything other than wonder at Jesus's goodness?

But then God quietly convicts me and I'm reminded of the sin in my own life. How often do I hold tighter to my "rules" than to the transformative truth of who Jesus is? How much of my time is dedicated to abstaining from sin so I can simply feel good about myself? How often do I fall into the sneaky trap of legalism?

If I had to guess, I'd say that legalism (trying to earn the favor of God) plays a part in all of our stories. We all probably have a list of rules or behavioral standards we've set for ourselves. Although righteousness is a positive trait for a Christian to have, legalism warps these rules into measurements of how close or distant we are from God.

Legalism rears its ugly head in moments when you...

+ *Feel more spiritual than the people around you because you've done your quiet time multiple days in a row*
+ *Judge your friend for going "too far" with her boyfriend when she knows better*
+ *Condemn your leaders when they say something that you don't agree with*
+ *Feel less holy because you listened to country radio instead of worship music in the car*
+ *Hate yourself after falling victim to that sin you swore you'd never repeat again*

+ Name some other moments when legalism has shown up in your life.

All of these moments make us believe the nasty lie that we have to do all the right things to earn God's love. We're either saying "Hey God! Check out all this impressive stuff I do or choose not to do for You" or "God, there's no way You could love me because of what I keep getting wrong."

On the flip side of this lie is the gospel truth: there is nothing we could ever do to earn God's saving favor. If we know, love, and choose His son then we *have* God's favor—forever! It's that simple.

The Pharisees were blind to the fact that Jesus was *Logos*, the living Word of God. His eventual sacrifice on the cross would give all people the invitation into freedom—freedom from legalism. Instead of putting ourselves in right standing with God through numbly checking off a list of rules and good deeds, we find righteousness in the person and love of Christ.

I love the response that Jesus gave to the Pharisees' persecution:

In his defense Jesus said to them, "My Father is always at his work to this very day, and I too am working."
John 5:17

Jesus didn't defend Himself, or even address the Law with which the Pharisees were so concerned. **He simply pointed to His relationship with the Father.** Jesus is saying: *"Wherever My Father is, that's where I'll be too."*

Jesus knows that our freedom, joy, and sanctification comes from our relationship with Him and with God, not our own ability to follow a set of rules.

So what does this mean for you and me?

Relationship over rules.

It's only through an authentic relationship with the Lord that we find the strength to say no to sin, let go of others' opinions, and trust that God will love us even if we fall short of what we believed to be our best. Instead of aiming for perfection, we should seek out God's heart in all situations and walk in His way just like Jesus did.

Go ahead and read the rest of John 5.

+ Take note of any details that stand out to you about the relationship between God the Father and Jesus.

"You are busy analyzing the Scriptures, frantically poring over them in hopes of gaining eternal life. Everything you read points to me, yet you still refuse to come to me so I can give you the life you're looking for—eternal life!"

John 5:39-40 TPT

I love the way that Jesus summed things up. It's as though He's saying, *"Look up child! Let go of your rules, your good deeds, and your striving and simply come to Me. In Me you'll find everything you need to faithfully carry out a life that honors God."*

AMEN! How freeing is that?! **Because of Jesus we are not in bondage to anything.** Legalism and perfection won't earn us anything, and sin will never have a hold on us. It's through our relationship with Jesus that we are able to walk in total freedom from any sin—joyfully obedient, and full of life in the Holy Spirit.

When we pick back up in John 6, Jesus is back in Galilee (this guy travels a lot!) and there is a whole crowd following Him because of the miracles He had performed. Jesus and the disciples were faced with the problem of trying to feed this large crowd of people. You've probably heard about the miracle of the feeding of the five thousand before, but here are a couple of fun facts you may have missed:

1. Other than the resurrection, this is the only miracle of Jesus recorded in ALL FOUR GOSPELS! (It must be pretty important!)

2. The number 5,000 technically only counted the men. If you included women and children, the total number could be more than 20,000 people who were fed that day! *WHOA*.

Reading through verse 14, we see that Jesus managed to feed at least 5,000 people with only five barley loaves and two small fish. The people who were there were astounded at this miracle of Jesus. They were low-key freaking out and fangirling over Him and honestly, I probably would be too.

So, what does Jesus do? Fill in the blanks below (v. 15).

Jesus, knowing that they intended to come and make him king by force, _____ again to a mountain _____ _____ .

The crowd was going wild for Jesus—but He didn't want their promotion. In a world that glorifies following and attention, Jesus chose the prize of His Father's presence over the praises of man. That speaks to my heart so much! My heart so often chooses worldly satisfaction rather than the deeper satisfaction that can only be found in the Lord.

Okay, let's keep moving it along though! In verses 26-29, we read that Jesus walked on water to catch back up with His disciples (Uh, no biggie...)! The next morning the crowds realized that Jesus had left that part of the lake, so they went off in search of Him. When they found Jesus, He called them out:

"Very truly I tell you, you are looking for me, not because you saw the signs I performed but because you ate the loaves and had your fill. Do not work for food that spoils, but for food that endures to eternal life, which the Son of Man will give you. For on him God the Father has placed his seal of approval."

Then they asked him, "What must we do to do the works God requires?"

Jesus answered, "The work of God is this: to believe in the one he has sent."
John 6:26b-29

Once again, these people were trapped in the nasty cycle of trying to earn God's favor. Jesus gave them the simple answer: *If you want to honor God well, trust Me.*

Jesus didn't tell them to *do* anything, but to simply trust. If we want to do the work of God, it begins with trusting Jesus. God is asking you and me to place our relationship with His Son at the center of our hearts. That's the only way we can receive an un-returnable invitation into the Kingdom and the heart of God.

I think about my own family and how my dad immediately loves and accepts anyone I bring home. He never stops to question whether they are worthy of his love and attention. He simply loves them because I love them. The same goes with God the Father! When you embrace His Son, you get God's love, favor, and attention forever.

Don't be like the critics of Jesus who were so distracted trying to "earn" the love of God that they missed the free invitation into a relationship with the Son. Look for the ways that legalism has snuck into your heart and life. Stop letting your rules be your God. Focus on your relationship with the One who can sustain you and nourish your heart forever.

"I speak to you living truth: Unite your heart to me and believe—and you will experience eternal life! I am the true Bread of Life."

John 6:47 TPT

Close out this week by reading the rest of John 6 on your own time.

my WHEN YOU'RE TIRED OF TRYING SO HARD story

sarah caison

Hi! My name is Sarah, and this is my *"When You're Tired of Trying So Hard"* story!

Like so many of you, much of my college career has centered around worship events, prayer meetings, Bible studies, and endless coffee dates. These are good things that honor the Lord and I truly believe He loves our participation! But for me, somewhere along the line I started believing that this wasn't "enough" for God.

I began adding silly rules and regulations in my life in order to be better for the Lord, restricting myself from so many things in order to become "holier." I could *only* listen to worship music. I could *only* hang out with people who radically loved Jesus. And I considered all television and movies to come straight from Satan himself (#crazygirl).

I thought I was becoming a "better Christian" but in all honesty, my list of holier-than-thou rules were ultimately a cover-up, masking the fear I felt of losing my salvation because of not doing enough. I allowed this anxiety to shape my relationship with the Lord. I believed that if didn't follow these rules, He would be upset with me.

"It is the Sabbath; the law forbids you to carry your mat."

John 5:10b

Similar to the Jewish leaders, I had taken my own interpretation of following God and added all of these extra checklist items. The posture of my heart became more about me and what I could do to secure my salvation and rightful place in the Kingdom rather than making my heart more like Jesus. **I became obsessed with following these little rules instead of fixing my eyes on the real ruler.**

In this season, I experienced a great deal of loneliness—I distanced myself from community because I seriously felt holier than them *(ouch, this is ugly)*. There was so much rotten fruit in this labor. It was hurting others and leading them further away—rather than closer to—God's heart. My heart aches as I write this because it shows the failure of human striving. No number of rules that we set up for ourselves will make us better. We will fail and fall into these legalistic tendencies if our hearts aren't postured toward our precious King.

Jesus responded to the religious leaders...

"Truly, truly, I say to you, whoever hears my word and believes him who sent me has eternal life. He does not come into judgment, but has passed from death to life."

John 5:24

Wow! According to Jesus, it's so simple: believe in Him. We must keep this as our focus in order to be freed from perfectionism, anxiety, fear, and guilt. When He is the focus, when He is what our souls cry out for—everything changes.

It is a lie that our own righteousness can make us better Christians. **We can never secure our position with the Lord by the things we do or by the rules that we follow.** This legalism makes us work harder to be loved and requires us to make more and more rules to ensure we cannot fall away. In doing this, our hearts are led astray and we end up lonely, desperate, and insecure.

Legalism exhausts us as we work to attain right standing with God—but as Romans 2:4 tells us, the kindness of God is what leads us to repentance. It is His loving kindness that shows us our right place at the foot of the cross. Our right place is falling before Him in repentance. We can let go of religious perfectionism by actively delighting in Christ's love, instead of working to attain it. May we ask each day where our hearts are postured and what motivates us!

CONVERSATION STARTERS

+ What did you learn about Jesus's character in John 5-6? It can be something new that you realized or something you were reminded of.

_____

_____

_____

_____

_____

_____

_____

+ Be honest with yourself. Have you tried to "earn" God's love in the past?

_____

_____

_____

_____

_____

+ What shape does legalism most often take in your life?
> + **Pride:** _because you get it right and it feels like other people are falling short._
> + **Overwhelming shame:** _because you fall short of your rules or expectations._
> + **A combination of the two:** _seasons of pride, followed by seasons of shame._

_____

_____

_____

+ How has legalism affected your relationship with God? How does it affect your relationship with the people around you?

_____

_____

_____

_____

_____

_____

_____

_____

_____

_____

_____

_____

+ What are some practical ways that you can place more focus on your relationship with Jesus over fixating on the "rules?"

_____

_____

_____

_____

_____

_____

_____

_____

_____

_____

_____

DELIGHT DATE IDEA

Because of Jesus we are not in bondage to anything; not to legalism and perfectionism, which won't earn us anything, and not to sin, which will never have a hold on us. It's through our relationship with Jesus that we are able to walk in total freedom from any sin, joyfully obedient, and full of life in the Holy Spirit.

Share with your Delight date about your own struggles with legalism. When have you fallen short of your own rules and expectations? When have you been prideful because you did follow your own rules and expectations? Talk together about what it looks like to live on the other side of bondage from legalism and sin. Celebrate this truth together over a sweet treat or your fave coffee drink!

MY DELIGHT DATE'S NAME: _____

DATE/TIME/PLACE: _____
_____

HOW I CAN BE PRAYING FOR MY DELIGHT DATE:
_____
_____
_____
_____

OTHER NOTES: _____
_____
_____
_____
_____

don't be so busy trying to earn the **LOVE OF GOD** that you miss the **FREE INVITATION** into a relationship with his son.

WHEN YOU'RE WALKING IN DARKNESS

John 7-9

We ended last week examining legalism, looking at Jewish leaders' negative views of Jesus and His new upside-down Kingdom doctrine. It seemed they had a problem with every single thing that Jesus said or did. This week, we're starting in John 7—it picks up with Jesus traveling all throughout Galilee, avoiding the province of Judea because of the Jewish leaders and their plot to have Him killed. If you ask me, that sounds terrifying! But David Guzik's *The Enduring Word* commentary clarifies that Jesus didn't avoid Jerusalem because He was afraid of His fate—rather, He was aware of His Father's perfect timing and plan. He waited patiently for God to speak and give Him the green light to go.

In John 7:2, we find out that the Feast of Tabernacles (tabernacle is just a fancy word for tent) was quickly approaching. The disciples tried to convince Jesus to go to the feast by reminding Him that He would never be successful or famous if He remained hidden. Jesus simply reminded them that His time had not come yet and urged them to go on without Him.

SIDE NOTE: *The Feast of Tabernacles was a weeklong camping partaaaayyyyy! The Jewish people would camp in and around Jerusalem in wooden booths made out of branches and leaves in remembrance of God's faithfulness to Israel in the wilderness after their departure from Egypt* (The Enduring Word).

But wait—plot twist! Even though He told the disciples He wasn't attending, Jesus still secretly went to the festival. When He arrived, the talk of the town was none other than Jesus Himself, and the city was abuzz with wonder about this extraordinary man. Some were for Him, while others were against Him. Halfway through the feast, Jesus surprised everyone by showing up in the temple and teaching.

This week we're going to zero in on a specific moment from this sermon, as Jesus spoke light and life into a woman who was an outcast in her society. We will read one of His seven famous "I am" statements: **"I am the Light of the World."** My prayer is that these ancient words of Jesus ring true in our own hearts and start to infiltrate the darkness that so many of us feel in our own lives.

Go read John 7 on your own.

Now, we're going to pick back up in John 8 after the feast is over. Jesus had stayed in Jerusalem and showed back up in the temple courts to teach again at dawn. In an attempt to embarrass Jesus and trip Him up, the Pharisees brought Him a woman who had been caught in the act of adultery.

I LOVE THIS STORY SO MUCH! Jesus is such a boss.

Pause and read John 8:1-11.

Can you imagine how this woman must have felt in this moment? Caught in the act of adultery, one of the most intimate sins, and forced out in front of a judgmental crowd. It's more than likely she wasn't wearing much clothing, probably trying to cover up her nakedness in more ways than one. I can almost picture the tears streaming down her face and the look of fear in her eyes at this moment of *excruciating* public shame.

I wonder what was going on in the backstory of her life. Had she and her husband been fighting? Was she feeling insecure and unloved? Was she reaching for anything to fill the deep void she felt in her life? Had the Pharisees tricked her into this act in order to question Jesus? John doesn't reveal these answers, but it makes me realize that so often, sin in my life has a deeper story in my heart. It typically stems from an unkempt place of brokenness and darkness.

+ I want you to notice Jesus's initial response. What does verse 6 say that Jesus did?

He bent down. Other translations say that He stooped down. Instead of responding with a verbal reprimand or correction, He simply paused, and postured Himself in a place of lowliness. He got on the same level as the adulterous woman. These men were trying to trap Jesus into condemning her, and instead, Jesus met her with quiet yet powerful grace in the midst of her shame and embarrassment.

Ugghhhh. This is why I *LOVE* Jesus.

While stooped down, Jesus wrote something in the dirt with His finger. What did He write? We don't exactly know. The Pharisees kept pressing Him to respond. He straightened back up and said, "Let any one of you who is without sin be the first to throw a stone at her" (v. 7). Then He returned to His position tracing something in the dirt.

Slowly but surely, one by one, the Pharisees and the rest of the crowd walked away. After some time, all who remained were Jesus and the adulterous woman. He stood back up, looked her in the eyes, spoke shocking grace with no condemnation, and encouraged her to go and sin no more.

Okay, so…excuse me while I full on ugly cry over here at this powerful moment between Jesus and this woman. Maybe my super intense emotional response comes from the fact that I relate to this woman in so many ways. No, I've never been caught in the act of adultery; but I've been caught so many times falling short of how I planned to carry out my love for God. When those things happen, I heap shame upon shame on my shoulders and walk around waiting for someone to condemn me and confirm the self-deprecating words I've been repeating to myself over and over. Maybe you've been there too.

I don't think it's by any accident that the very next verse immediately following this story is John 8:12. Fill in the blanks below:

When Jesus spoke again to the people, he said, "I am the _____ of the_____.
Whoever follows me will never walk in _____, but will have the _____ of life."

After such a public ordeal, I'm not sure if the woman was still present, listening as Jesus continued teaching—but I'd like to think she was there in the back, smiling as He spoke these simple yet profound words to her and to her accusers.

What sticks out to me is that Jesus was more interested in giving her His light than He was in condemning her for her darkness. If you've been walking around in shame and wondering what Jesus's response to your brokenness is, here it is...

He says, *"I am the Light of the World. If you're walking in darkness, come to Me and sin no more."*

Because of Jesus, we don't have to fear the darkness (but I know that's easier said than done). We all face darkness, emptiness, hardship, pain, loss, heartache, and heaviness on a daily basis. Some of you have sicknesses in your families, others of you feel like you don't have any real friends. You're walking through severe anxiety and depression, or you're away from home where your parents have been fighting. Perhaps you're struggling in your classes, you've just had your heart broken, or you're dealing with insecurity every day.

Listen—*I know how it goes. Sometimes it feels like the darkness is winning.* To be honest, I feel the weight of darkness on a lot of days and I talk to a lot of other girls who do too. **But we can take courage in the universal truth that the only thing powerful enough to make the darkness disappear is light.**

Light is the answer to darkness! Remember this from John 1? Jesus is the embodiment of light and life. His light shines the brightest in the darkest of places, which means we don't have to fear the darkness in our lives—we walk hand in hand with the Light of the World.

I'd be willing to bet that a lot of us relate to the woman caught in adultery. We're ashamed of what we've done, what's in our past, the thoughts in our mind, or how we think we messed things up. We fixate on the darkness rather than moving toward the light. But I think God is extending an invitation to us all to simply lock our eyes on the light of Jesus. His light and His voice can and will lead us out of the darkness, overpowering whatever we face. All we have to do is move toward Him.

Picture yourself there on the ground, in the dirt, attempting to cover your nakedness, surrounded by enemies and accusers. That sin you've been so desperate to hide is now sitting in the light for all to see.

Now imagine, this man Jesus speaks, and one by one your accusers start to fall back until you and Jesus are the only ones left. Even with your head down, you can see Him stooped down in the dirt near you, paying no attention to the thing of which you're so ashamed. He rises, and as His body lifts you feel your body start to lift too—like a mirror image. He looks you in the eyes and asks, "Where are your accusers? Is there no one here to condemn you?"

As you look around at the empty scene, no one is more surprised than you to find that every single accuser has left. You quietly whisper back, "I see no one, Lord."

With kind eyes and strength in His voice He says, "Then I certainly don't condemn you either. Go, and from now on, be free from a life of sin" (John 8:11 TPT).

Darkness has no hold on you. Sin will not win. You walk with the Light of the World!

Go ahead and finish reading John 8 and 9. Take note of how Jesus continues to speak light and freedom into everyone He encounters.

my WHEN YOU'RE WALKING IN DARKNESS story
jordan smith

Hi! My name is Jordan, and this is my *"When You're Walking in Darkness"* story!

I don't know about you, but *WOW*—that story of Jesus and the woman caught in adultery brings me such peace and comfort. To hear Jesus say that He is the Light of the World, and whoever walks with Him will never have to walk in darkness, just allows me to take a big sigh of relief in knowing that I am not alone.

At the end of my senior year of high school, I received the worst news of my life. My father was diagnosed with stage 4 lung cancer, and my world came crashing down. My parents were divorced, so I began the summer before college by taking care of the man who had taken care of me for the last 18 years. Many had told me to go to church and build my relationship with the Lord, but I was so hurt by God. How could this happen to me? How could this be my dad? Surely God didn't care about my family or me if He had made my father so sick... Thoughts like this consumed my mind.

Two days before my first day of college, my dad's twin sister called me, crying hysterically, letting me know that my dad had passed away to be with Jesus. My heart was shattered; broken. *How? Why?* That day was the darkest day of my life. I didn't get out of bed, I couldn't move—I was numb.

School started the very next Monday, and my mom assured me that taking a semester off was not an option, that my dad wouldn't have allowed it. My first weeks were hopelessly dark. Because I commuted to school, I was very alone. I would go to parties to cope with the pain and the loss of my dad. My mom saw the path I was headed down and encouraged me to get involved in a sorority on campus. Before I knew it, recruitment had arrived. The day I accepted a bid was the same day I met my best friend, Hope.

I opened up about the loss of my father to Hope and my sorority sisters at a freshman retreat. Afterward, a girl came up to me and asked if I would be interested in going to church with her. I assured her that, again, my dad had already passed away—if I was ever going to go to church and have a relationship with Jesus, I should have done it back in May when my dad was diagnosed.

But the next night, Hope and I went back to our dorms and shared every detail of our lives and our faith with each other. We both decided that we didn't want to continue the lifestyles we had chosen; drinking and partying were not filling either of us up, leading us to a better life, or fulfilling the missing pieces we needed.

Over Christmas break that year, I began my walk with the Lord. Jesus sat with me and put my broken heart back together. He assured me that my earthly father was out of pain and healed, and although my earthly father couldn't be with me anymore, my heavenly Father would be. My heavenly Father would be there in the car with me after a long day of work, would dine with me and go to coffee dates with me, and would be there for me when I walked down the aisle.

The Bible became my sword, and any time the enemy tried to whisper lies about the loss of my dad, God's Word came to life with a beautiful explanation of His goodness and Jesus's love. My dark days were fewer and fewer as my chains were broken and I was set free. Darkness no longer had a hold on my life.

You see, God knows every detail of your life. He understands your heartbreak after the loss of a loved one, the pain of a breakup, the struggle to love a challenging family member, and even the masking of loneliness through drugs, alcohol, and sex. He sees *every* area of your darkness and desires to be the light in your heart. He offers His love as a balm for *every* wound you have.

The woman caught in adultery never expected Jesus to meet her right where she was at, to love on her, or to allow her to walk away and leave her life of sin. This isn't just good news for her—it's REALLY good news for us! Jesus is saying the same thing to you, sis. He doesn't call us to live in shame and guilt, He wants us to walk free. Whatever you are suffering through, you are not called to do it alone. Jesus wants to walk this journey of life with you and guide you with the light of His Word.

CONVERSATION STARTERS

+ What did you learn about Jesus's character in John 7-9? It can be something new that you realized or something you were reminded of.

_____

_____

_____

_____

_____

_____

_____

_____

_____

_____

_____

+ Who do you relate to more in the story and why?
> + **The adulterous woman:** _you feel trapped in a never-ending cycle of sin and shame._
> + **The Pharisees:** _you are tempted to judge and condemn those around you for the places they fall short._

_____

_____

_____

_____

_____

_____

_____

+ What darkness are you currently walking through in your life?

_____

_____

_____

_____

_____

_____

+ How do you currently feel Jesus meeting you in your darkness? What are some of the small slivers of light you can identify?

_____

_____

_____

_____

_____

_____

_____

_____

_____

_____

_____

+ What can you do to start walking away from the darkness and toward the light that Jesus offers?

_____

_____

_____

_____

_____

_____

_____

DELIGHT DATE IDEA

So many of us relate to the women caught in adultery—we're embarrassed of our sin and afraid to let others see our nakedness. Spend time with your Delight date this week simply punching holes in the darkness.

Share one thing (it can be super small or something bigger) that you've been ashamed to tell someone. Maybe it's something you said, something you did, or something you didn't do. Whatever it is, meet each other with open arms and sit in the glorious light of Jesus together.

MY DELIGHT DATE'S NAME: _____

DATE/TIME/PLACE: _____
_____

HOW I CAN BE PRAYING FOR MY DELIGHT DATE:
_____
_____
_____
_____

OTHER NOTES: _____
_____
_____
_____
_____

when jesus spoke
again to the
people, he said,
"I AM THE
LIGHT OF
THE WORLD.
whoever follows
me will never
walk in darkness,
but will have the
LIGHT OF LIFE."

john 8:12

WHEN YOU'RE WAITING ON GOD

John 10-12

I may or may not still be in tears from last week's study of the encounter between Jesus and the adulterous woman. That moment will always cut me deep, but it's time to dry my tears and keep moving through the book of John! I have been looking forward to this section for a while, and I'm pumped about what God will reveal to us through His Word this week. We're going to read John 11 and 12 together and look at Jesus's relationship with a well-known family in Scripture: Mary, Martha, and Lazarus of Bethany.

You've probably read about the death and resurrection of Lazarus (sorry for the spoiler) before, but I want us to look at this story through a slightly different lens. My hope and prayer is that you might find peace for your own waiting heart as we reflect on this story.

SIDE NOTE: *Due to a lack of time, we're going to skip reading John 10 together—but I urge you to spend some time* *reading it on your own. It offers such a beautiful picture of Jesus as our watchful Good Shepherd. There is so much gold in these 42 verses, including one of my most favorite passages in the whole Bible: John 10:10-11! Read it in The Passion Translation for a powerful reminder of the life found in Jesus.*

Okay, let's do this! Open up that Bible and turn to John 11.

Now a man named Lazarus was sick. He was from Bethany, the village of Mary and her sister Martha. (This Mary, whose brother Lazarus now lay sick, was the same one who poured perfume on the Lord and wiped his feet with her hair.) So the sisters sent word to Jesus, "Lord, the one you love is sick."

When he heard this, Jesus said, "This sickness will not end in death. No, it is for God's glory so that God's Son may be glorified through it." Now Jesus loved Martha and her sister and Lazarus. So when he heard that Lazarus was sick, he stayed where he was two more days.

John 11:1-7

In this story we meet Mary, Martha, and Lazarus. Luke 10:38-42 gives us a look into how their friendship might have begun, so flip there if you're curious about their backstory. In John 11 we find out that Lazarus, the brother of Mary and Martha, is extremely sick, almost to the point of death.

The sisters collectively sent a message to Jesus asking Him to come to Bethany. Notice how twice in verses 1-6, John tells us that **Jesus loved Mary, Martha, and Lazarus.** This relationship ran deep. I find it beautiful that Mary and Martha didn't make any specific request for healing or demand Jesus do something. They made Him aware of their need, extended Him an invitation, and trusted that because He loved and cared, He would respond appropriately. *(Umm, pro-tip for prayer, am I right?!)*

I want you to see this moment in your mind: Mary and Martha watching as their brother's health slowly declines, gradually growing weaker, the life draining from his once joy-filled face. They know that Jesus has the incredible power to heal, so in their most desperate moment, they send word to Him that Lazarus is ill. I can picture them quietly glancing to the door every few minutes, anxiously awaiting the arrival of the only one who could change the outcome of their situation.

But He didn't show.

Lazarus died and it seemed like all hope was lost.

Can you imagine how devastated Mary and Martha must have felt? They had a deeply personal relationship with this man who healed strangers, turned water into wine, made a feast out of a mere snack…and for some reason, He didn't show up for them. Personally, I would be *beyond* disappointed.

Skip ahead to verse 17 and let's see how the sisters responded to Jesus being a no-show.

On his arrival, Jesus found that Lazarus had already been in the tomb for four days. Now

Bethany was less than two miles from Jerusalem, and many Jews had come to Martha and Mary to comfort them in the loss of their brother. When Martha heard that Jesus was coming, she went out to meet him, but Mary stayed at home.

"Lord," Martha said to Jesus, "if you had been here, my brother would not have died. But I know that even now God will give you whatever you ask."
John 11:17-22

Okay—let's take note of a couple of things here.

1. Lazarus had been dead for FOUR days when Jesus arrived. That's four days of mourning, bitterness, and confusion. One could imagine that Mary and Martha had *all the feels* at this point.

2. I want you to notice that Mary stayed in the house. This might not seem like a big deal, but let's remember from the story in Luke 10 that Mary was the spirited sister. She wanted to be around Jesus ALL the time and had no problem leaving behind her obligations to be with Him. I think her choice to stay home was a very intentional statement about her feelings toward Jesus in that moment.

3. Martha went out to meet Jesus as He entered Bethany. I can almost hear the crushing disappointment in her voice as she said to Him, "If you had been here, my brother would not have died." I think we all can relate to Martha's response—it seems to me that was her way of passive-aggressively saying, *"What the heck, Jesus? Where were You?!"*

Lazarus died and Jesus waited. John 11:5-6 tells us that He waited two whole days before getting up and going to Bethany. This doesn't seem like the actions you'd expect from a very good friend who is caring, compassionate, and loving. The mark of a good friend is usually a willingness to drop everything to be there for you at a moment's notice. So what kind of Savior would wait *two days* during such a crisis? Like didn't Jesus understand that His friends were anxious and terrified? Didn't He care about Lazarus? Why had He waited?

Let's check out what was happening with Jesus while Mary and Martha were waiting. Go ahead and read John 11:6-16 on your own.

Jesus was with His disciples in Galilee and announced His intention to go back to Judea. As we've learned from our previous weeks together, this was a dangerous move because the Jewish leaders in Judea were plotting to have Him killed.

Jesus announced to the disciples that Lazarus was dead, and they were going to wake him up. I'm sure the disciples thought something like, *"This guy is crazy!"* Hadn't they just watched Jesus wait for two days after He received word of Lazarus's sickness? Now He wanted to go, when the guy had already died?! Not to mention—Jesus would probably be the next one to die if He returned to Judea.

But don't you love how Jesus always did things His way? With Mary and Martha, Jesus waited when they wanted Him to go, and with the disciples He went when they wanted Him to wait. I know from my own life experience that God doesn't play games with me. He's a God of clarity and peace, but if I'm being honest, His timing sometimes frustrates me.

I have to actively remind myself that His ways are not our ways, and His timing is not always our timing. The path of Jesus doesn't always make sense in our rational brains, but His plan is always SO much greater than anything we could rationally fathom. With this in mind, I can only imagine that Jesus was doing something of the utmost importance in His waiting.

When Jesus finally arrived in Bethany, He comforted Martha with the words, "Your brother will rise and live." Jesus had total confidence in what was about to happen. He then sent Martha to bring Mary to Him and she fell at His feet in mourning. Jesus burst into tears at the sight of His friend Mary and the community of Bethany in grief.

Then we get one of the shortest verses in the entire Bible.

Fill in the blanks:

"_____ _____."

John 11:35

Let's read John 11:41-44 together and see what happened to Lazarus after Jesus convinced the mourners to roll away the stone in front of the tomb.

So they took away the stone. Then Jesus looked up and said, "Father, I thank you that you have heard me. I knew that you always hear me, but I said this for the benefit of the people standing here, that they may believe that you sent me."

When he had said this, Jesus called in a loud voice,

"Lazarus, come out!" The dead man came out, his hands and feet wrapped with strips of linen, and a cloth around his face.

Jesus said to them, "Take off the grave clothes and let him go."

Notice the prayer that Jesus prayed when the stone was rolled away. He didn't pray that He would now have the power to raise Lazarus. He thanked the Father for hearing Him. You see, *His prayer had already been answered!*

SIDE NOTE: *In the verses prior to this prayer, Martha challenged Jesus not to remove the stone because of the raunchy smell from a four-day-old dead body that had sat above ground in the warm Judean climate. When the stone was rolled away, I think Jesus immediately knew that Lazarus was not dead because there was no smell. Lazarus was simply sleeping! Jesus only needed to call him out of the tomb and the miracle would be complete.*

So, back to Jesus's prayer. It reveals what Jesus had done during those two days of waiting in Galilee: He talked to His Father. In those two silent days on the other side of the Jordan river, Jesus prayed for this outcome, for resurrection life for Lazarus, and for what would happen through it. When they took the stone away, Jesus's two-day prayer had been answered.

In Mary and Martha's waiting, *Jesus was working.*

While Mary and Martha were bitter about Jesus not showing up, *Jesus was talking to the Father.*

When it felt like all hope had been lost, *Jesus was just getting started.*

And how crazy is this: that's OUR Jesus too! In our waiting, Jesus is working.

When we're bitter because it seems like Jesus isn't showing up, *Jesus is talking to the Father on our behalf.* When it feels like all hope has been lost, *Jesus is just getting started.*

Maybe you're in a season of waiting in your own life. Perhaps you're waiting to figure out your future, waiting on friends, waiting for a relationship, waiting for that person who hurt you to apologize, waiting for an opportunity, or waiting for your breakthrough.

Whatever it is that we're waiting on, let's not forget that Jesus is moving in more ways than we know. In our culture of instant gratification—via Instagram, fast passes, mobile ordering, drive-thru windows, etc.—waiting seems to go against the grain of everything we know. Sometimes waiting even feels like a punishment rather than a gift to be treasured. The story of Lazarus reminds us that our waiting is actually a beautiful opportunity to see the glory of Jesus on display in our lives. It's through our waiting that we build faith and trust in Jesus and His plans for our lives.

Yes, that is a *serious* perspective shift for the things that we just can't wait to have an answer about! But rather than seeing our waiting as a punishment, let's praise and trust God because we KNOW He's working on our behalf. I don't know about you, but from now on I only want an answer when I know it's being given in His timing. I want to be just like Jesus as He waited in Galilee—on my knees in prayer, talking to my Father in heaven before I take a single step in any direction. **God knows what we need, and if He wants us to wait, we can trust that it's for our good and for His glory.**

On the other side of the tomb, Mary and Martha saw that their wait was 1,000% worth it. In John 12, we see that Mary went on to anoint the feet of Jesus with a pint of extremely expensive perfume at a dinner honoring Him. I wonder if that was her way of fully committing her life to the ways, words, and works of Jesus, worshipping Him with everything that she had, and trusting His timing and control in her life. This act of worship was Mary's proclamation that she would wait at the feet of Jesus. Let's make that our proclamation too—we will wait at the feet of Jesus, worshipping Him with everything we have!

Finish out this week by reading John 12 on your own and pay attention to how Jesus responded to Mary's worshipful act of devotion.

my WHEN YOU'RE WAITING ON GOD story
margaret hoyt

Hi! My name is Margaret, and this is my *"When You're Waiting on God"* story.

I can 100% relate to Mary and Martha from the story of Lazarus—expecting Jesus to do one thing, waiting with total frustration, and finding out on the other side that the way of Jesus is *always* better.

When I pictured college, I pictured the perfect friend group. You know the ones; they road trip together every weekend, they have choreographed dances, they know all the words to the same songs, they take really cute pictures, and they show up for each other every time without fail. I pictured having four best friends and road-tripping back home with them for every holiday. I waited...and waited...and waited...for those friends to show up.

During my first two years at school, I was chasing after God harder than I ever had before. I was attending Bible studies and Delight, journaling every day, and going to church every Sunday. I found so much abundance in my life with the Lord. He was opening my eyes to so many cool things He had been doing, and yet I was consistently met with loneliness and impatience when it came to my friendships.

I kept holding on to this promise I had made in my head that if I chased after God, He would give me the perfect group of girls to pursue Him with. I continued to wait...I went on coffee dates, I studied with random girls, and I still came up empty. Don't get me wrong, I definitely enjoyed those coffee dates and hangs, but I still hadn't found *the* friends I was waiting for.

Finally, I gave up. I threw in the towel and didn't know where to go or who to turn to. Eventually I turned to Jesus with my frustration, pleading with Him and trying to make deals (how ridiculous, I know). I was frustrated that God hadn't pulled His weight in my plan, hadn't showed up the way I thought He would, and didn't seem to be hearing my prayers or requests.

I love how in the story from John 11, when Jesus finally arrived, He met Mary and Martha in their mess and mourning. Jesus did the same for me. He met me in the place where it hurt the most. He wept with me, like He wept with them. He met me despite the blame I had placed on Him from my confusion over His timing. He met me with grace because He knew I couldn't see what He had been up to all along. Jesus showed me what He had been working on and opened my eyes to the beauty of the friendships that were just ahead of me—if I could trust Him with my waiting.

Jesus rolled away the stones that were in front of my eyes and showed me the joy on the other side of trust. Slowly but surely, those friendships came. Guess what? They looked absolutely *nothing* like I expected! Instead of one friend group that I did absolutely everything with, I developed several amazing friendships in my life with people who poured into me in so many different ways.

I realized that in my impatience, God had been planting seeds that would grow into amazing friendships. It's like when you go to a Mexican restaurant and you pig out on the chips and salsa rather than waiting for the far more satisfying fajitas or quesadilla you ordered. I wanted instant gratification served with instantaneous friends as soon as I got to college. But in asking me to wait longer, God gave me relationships that I believe will satisfy my heart for years and years to come.

Instead of driving across the country with friends like I had expected my freshman year, I took a flight across the world to see my best friend who lived abroad. Instead of the constant photo shoots I had dreamt up before, I took once-in-a-lifetime photos of my friend getting engaged. Instead of the big group events I had wanted to attend, I cherish the memories of living in a home with my best friend.

I'm so thankful for my waiting season because I now see how it prepared my heart for what God had in mind. Maybe you're starting to grow impatient over something in your own life. I challenge you to change your perspective. What if you chose to celebrate the waiting and trust that God sees the bigger picture? Waiting on God won't always be easy (in fact, it never is) but we can trust that His ways are always better. After all, He knows our hearts' desires better than anyone! We can trust Him with every second, minute, and hour of our days.

CONVERSATION STARTERS

+ What did you learn about Jesus's character in John 10-12?
It can be something new that you realized or something you
were reminded of.

_____

_____

_____

_____

_____

_____

_____

_____

_____

+ When you're in a season of waiting, how do you typically
respond when things don't go the way you want them to?

> **+ More like Martha:** *you run to Jesus but hold quiet
> bitterness in your heart because He didn't move in
> the way you expected.*
> **+ More like Mary:** *you hold Jesus at arm's length and
> avoid Him because of your disappointment.*
> *+ Fill in the blank with any other way you might
> respond to waiting on the Lord.*

_____

_____

_____

_____

_____

_____

+ Identify something in your life that you're currently frustrated about having to wait on.

_____

_____

_____

_____

_____

_____

_____

_____

_____

+ How did this week's Scripture encourage you to change your posture toward seasons of waiting in your life? What do you want to do differently in the future?

_____

_____

_____

_____

_____

_____

_____

_____

_____

_____

_____

DELIGHT DATE IDEA

Read and discuss Mary and Martha's backstory from Luke 10:38-42 with your Delight date. How did their posture toward Jesus change from the story in Luke to the story in John? In what ways do you relate with these two women? Share about seasons of waiting that you both are currently in and how you're learning to trust God's timing.

MY DELIGHT DATE'S NAME: _____

DATE/TIME/PLACE: _____
_____

HOW I CAN BE PRAYING FOR MY DELIGHT DATE:
_____
_____
_____
_____

OTHER NOTES: _____
_____
_____
_____
_____
_____
_____
_____
_____
_____
_____
_____

God knows
what we need,
and if He
wants us
TO WAIT,
we can trust
that it's for
OUR GOOD
and for
HIS GLORY.

WHEN YOU'RE CALLED TO LOVE

John 13

Welcome to Week 6! We are already over halfway through the book of John, and this week we're going to see a major transition in our text. John (the author) wrote things a tad differently than the other gospel authors (Matthew, Mark, and Luke). John was less of a details guy and more of a "poetic moment" guy. He had a very specific purpose in his writing that directly influenced what he chose to include in his gospel account. Before we dive into the bulk of our text today, I want to fast forward to John 20 to zero in on his purpose for writing.

Jesus performed many other signs in the presence of his disciples, which are not recorded in this book. But these are written that you may believe that Jesus is the Messiah, the Son of God, and that by believing you may have life in his name.

John 20:30-31

In this verse, John gives us his thesis statement: *that you may believe.*

John chose very specific stories, signs, and moments from the life of Jesus to lead the reader to belief in who Jesus was (and is). Over the last 12 chapters, we've read about seven signs or miracles done by Jesus which John intentionally chose to lead readers to believe in Jesus.

THE SEVEN SIGNS IN JOHN
1. *Turning water into wine (John 2:1-12)*
2. *Healing a government official's son in Cana (John 4:46-54)*
3. *Healing the man at the pools of Bethesda (John 5:1-15)*
4. *Feeding the five thousand (John 6:1-15)*
5. *Walking on water on the Sea of Galilee (John 6:16-21)*
6. *Healing the blind man in Jerusalem (John 9:1-41)*
7. *Raising Lazarus from the dead (John 11:1-44)*

Last week's story about the death and resurrection of Lazarus marked the end of these seven signs. In this next section of our text, we're moving away from the public ministry of Jesus and into a very up-close and personal meeting between Jesus and the disciples. I love these next few chapters in John because they act as a **living love letter** from Jesus to those that He loved most. I'm sure every word spoke so deeply to the disciples in that upper room—just as I'm sure they will hit you intensely as you read them today. As you study these next few chapters, I want you to put yourself in the story, feel the weight of this conversation, and see how Jesus calls you to love deeper.

Let's start back up in John 13.

It was just before the Passover Festival. Jesus knew that the hour had come for him to leave this world and go to the Father. Having loved his own who were in the world, he loved them to the end.

John 13:1

Jesus knew that His time had come. The mission that His Father had sent Him to do was, within 24 hours or so, about to come to completion. I don't think it's by any accident that this moment in the upper room happened right before Passover. Passover was the greatest of all the Jewish festivals, commemorating the freedom of the Israelites from Egyptian captivity.

SIDE NOTE: *Need a memory jog about Passover? Remember the plagues and Moses begging Pharaoh to let God's people go in the book of Exodus? The tenth and final plague that ultimately led to Israel's freedom was God's promise to kill the firstborn son of every home including Pharaoh's. The Jewish people were told to sacrifice a lamb and place its blood over the entrance of their home, so that the plague would "pass over" and spare Hebrew sons.*

As the Passover celebration approached, Jesus knew that He would be the final Passover lamb, sacrificing His own life to save us all. These verses are His parting words to His disciples, those that would continue to carry out His mission and lay the foundation for the church we know today.

A parallel passage in Luke 22 tells us that these sacred moments between Jesus and the disciples happened in a guest room of a home that belonged to a follower of Jesus in Jerusalem. It was a furnished upstairs room that Jesus sent John and Peter to prepare ahead of time. During their Passover meal together, Jesus showed the ultimate sign of humility by washing the disciples' feet.

The evening meal was in progress, and the devil had already prompted Judas, the son of Simon Iscariot, to betray Jesus. Jesus knew that the Father had put all things under his power, and that he had come from God and was returning to God; so he got up from the meal, took off his outer clothing, and wrapped a towel around his waist. After that, he poured water into a basin and began to wash his disciples' feet, drying them with the towel that was wrapped around him.

John 13:2-5

Think about how crazy that decision was! Up until that moment, Jesus had been the shepherd leading the flock. He had done everything with total power and might—He was the disciples' fearless leader. They had seen Him calm the seas with the sound of His voice, outsmart the religious leaders of the day, and even bring the dead back to life. Perhaps that's why it was so shocking when He took on the lowest posture in the room, lowering Himself to the ground and washing the dirty feet of each disciple. I wonder if, as He washed their feet, He was thinking about the moment to come on the cross and how this humble action was a quiet declaration of His love for each one of them.

Peter, I love you. I would go to the very end of love for you.

Andrew, I love you. I would go to the very end of love for you.

Judas, I love you. I would go to the very end of love for you.

+ In verse 2, we find out which disciple was going to betray Jesus. Who is it?

Notice how evil crept into this tight-knit group at the very moment when the love of Jesus was on its fullest display yet. At that moment, Judas had already fallen victim to the suggested whispers of the enemy—yet Jesus still displayed His utmost love for Judas by washing his feet, even while knowing he was about to betray Him. That's powerful stuff!

In verse 3 we see the "why" behind Jesus's choice. Jesus didn't lower Himself into a posture of humility from a place of weakness, but rather from a position of all authority and confidence in His identity. It was His confidence in the love of the Father that led Jesus to this beautiful display of authentic love clothed in vulnerability and strength.

As you've probably already guessed, in Jewish culture it was typically the job of the least important person in the room to wash the feet of their superiors. It would be socially unacceptable for a teacher or a king to be seen washing the feet of others. Perhaps that's why Peter objected and declared that he wanted to wash the feet of Jesus instead.

But in that moment, Jesus was teaching the disciples a new definition of love—love that chooses sacrifice and is willing to get messy, up-close, and vulnerable for the sake of others. **In Jesus, we find a new way to love.** Jesus continued to wash Peter's feet and called him to step into this upside-down Kingdom love too.

When he had finished washing their feet, he put on his clothes and returned to his place. "Do you

understand what I have done for you?" he asked
them. "You call me 'Teacher' and 'Lord,' and rightly
so, for that is what I am. Now that I, your Lord
and Teacher, have washed your feet, you also
should wash one another's feet. I have set you an
example that you should do as I have done for you.
Very truly I tell you, no servant is greater than his
master, nor is a messenger greater than the one who
sent him. Now that you know these things, you will
be blessed if you do them."

John 13:12-17

If it were my last day on earth, I would be FREAKING
OUT. But rather than being preoccupied with thoughts
of His own death to come, Jesus spent His last day
100% consumed by His love for the disciples. His love is
mysterious yet personal; simple yet complex; challenging
yet gentle.

In our culture today, "love" has been watered down with
a million different definitions that make it hard for us to
understand the type of love that Jesus is showing us. We
love Jesus and we "love" tacos. We love our families and
we "love" celebrities. We love our church and we "love" our
local coffee shop. We use "love" to describe our admiration
for just about anything.

When it comes to people, we especially confuse the truth
of what love is. We tend to only give our love to those who
earn our love. If they offer something of value to us, we
think they deserve to be loved by us. We love and admire
those who do flashy and brilliant things in our world. We
put them on a pedestal, follow their lives on Instagram,

listen to their voices, and praise them for every new shiny thing they do. But this type of love doesn't require proximity. You can admire these people from afar without ever seeing the messy parts of their hearts and lives.

Jesus isn't talking about admiration or even adoration. He's talking about the kind of love that doesn't always add up and even out. It's the kind of love that would lead the Savior of the world to wash the feet of the very one who was getting ready to betray Him, asking for his love, yet leaving him the decision to ultimately accept or refuse.

The Jesus way of love means surrender, sacrifice, and selflessness. It happens in the trenches of relationships, not just on the mountaintops. That flies in the face of what so many of us think love looks like. I doubt many of us would be willing to admit it, but we often treat love less like Jesus and a bit more like Judas.

We love with conditions.
We love until we get a better offer.
We run away before anyone we love can hurt us.

After Jesus washed the feet of the disciples, He addressed Judas and gave him freedom to run toward what he thought he wanted. Read John 13:21-27.

This moment breaks my heart because I see how it hurts the heart of Jesus, and what's scary is that it almost feels like looking in a mirror. I've never wanted to see my own heart reflected in Judas but to be honest, I constantly choose Judas's version of love over Jesus's. I run toward temporary fixes, places of comfort, and shiny things instead of Jesus all the time. I wish I could sit here and judge Judas for his blatant rejection of Jesus—but that would be hypocritical of me. I am perhaps more like Judas than I thought, constantly basking in the love of Jesus yet hating His ways at the same time. Anybody else with me? (Don't worry! There is good news for those of us who are Judas doppelgängers.)

What I love about this heartbreaking moment is that Jesus's love shone even brighter set against the backdrop of Judas's rejection—so much so, that it created the perfect opportunity for Jesus to introduce a new commandment.

Go ahead and read the remainder of John 13.

+ What is the new commandment that Jesus gave the disciples? (v. 34)

Jesus left the disciples with one last commandment, which could fairly be called the heart and soul of His entire message and ministry. In the law of Moses from the Old Testament, the Hebrews were called to love God with all their heart, soul, and strength (Deut. 6:5) and to love their neighbor as themselves (Lev. 19:18). Here Jesus took it one step further, asking His disciples not only to love others as they loved themselves, but to love as He had loved them. That's a BIG difference.

The disciples just spent three years with Jesus seeing His love on display in every moment. Now they were charged with taking everything they saw and experienced and showing that same love to the world. To sum it all up, Jesus said, *"The proof of My love in you will be evidenced in your love for one another. That is how people will know who you follow."*

I want you to stop and think about how love shows up in your life. When is the last time someone experienced Jesus because of the way you loved them? When is the last time you went out of your way to love someone who had nothing to offer you? When was the last time love called you to humble yourself and sacrifice for someone else?

I'm guessing there is room for you, for me, and for all of us to step deeper into the Jesus way of love. This way gives not from a place of fear or the need to prove, but simply out of a heart for Jesus. It's a love that chooses messy communion, life-altering sacrifice, and risky vulnerability. We don't have to be like Judas, who ran away from the love of Jesus, chasing the next shiny thing. Let's be women who sink deeper into the love that Jesus has for us together and make Him more known by the way we show love to one another.

my WHEN YOU'RE CALLED TO LOVE story
colleen gill

Hi! My name is Colleen, and this is my *"When You're Called To Love"* story!

Sometime before I can truly even remember, I developed a nasty habit of confusing self-denial for love. I didn't trust love to be unconditional, so I did my best to make myself the fulfillment of every condition I thought that people might have. I thought I was being self-sacrificial, vulnerable even, but I was really just trying to control the way people loved me and the way I loved them in return. This control was supposed to give me the security I craved, but instead it almost took from me the most important person in my life: my sister.

Growing up, my sister was my best friend and my idol. I wanted nothing more than to be just like her one day. But, as Jesus knew and I later learned, relationships can be really messy. Early on in my high school career, my sister and I had a falling out that left me completely crushed.

After she moved away from home, I felt like I had lost her. Continued miscommunication and distance created a horrible cycle in which I isolated my feelings and she lashed out. To me, this rude awakening was a false confirmation of my beliefs about love. Satan used those moments to try and convince me that I was not worthy of being loved unconditionally—that I hadn't measured up enough to deserve her love. I decided the only answer was to completely stop talking to her. If I couldn't win her love, then it would be too painful to keep trying.

That false narrative of love started to seep into other relationships in my life. Even the best of my friendships still felt empty, off, and distant (although I tried to deny it at the time). I had stubbornly decided that I had made the right decision to not speak with my sister, but there was a part of me that longed for healing and a true intimacy with her. Surely there had to be more to love than whatever I had been living in!

I knew that something major needed to shift. I remember the moment vividly when things began to change. I went to the campus chapel with my mentor, and she challenged me to use our time to pray—to talk to God about my sister. It was the last thing I wanted to do. But God listened to my reluctant prayers.

As I talked to God, I realized that I had masked my hurt and my emptiness with anger and stubbornness for years. I felt convicted of my disbelief in the healing power of the love of God, as He revealed my own self-righteousness surrounding my anger. I felt that I was the one who had been hurt, and that I had the right to be angry for as long as I wanted. But something deeper in me than that anger desired to surrender. Sitting in the campus chapel that day, I prayed for hours. *God, please, will You help me to forgive, I don't want to be angry anymore, I don't want to hurt like this.*

As I was praying, I felt a physical weight lift from my shoulders, and it felt like I could breathe again. I thought about the truth of the gospel: how the Lord of creation died painfully to forgive me, and how I had been so comfortable in my self-righteous anger and pain that I was missing the point of it all.

Y'all, I had been condemning my sister for causing my pain for years, but the truth of the matter is that I was Judas the whole time. Judas, so good at making excuses for his sin, so confident that he had to look out for himself. I didn't trust God to love me, so I didn't really love anyone well in return. Loving my sister—loving anyone, for that matter—meant getting close enough to be hurt. I had refused to trust that there was a healer on the other side of my pain. I realized that the healing I so desperately needed could only come from up-close-and-personal tenderness and truth.

A couple of months after that revelation in the chapel, I flew across the country to spend a week with my sister. It had been several years since we had been together. I decided during that week to simply lean in, even when everything inside of me screamed to run from the possibility of pain. **But the truth is that love, true and sacrificial love, is redemptive.** We spent a lot of time restoring our relationship. She pushed me to love her vulnerably and to get messy. She all but washed my feet.

Jesus wasn't naïve—He washed Judas's feet knowing full well that His beloved friend was exchanging His life for money. When Jesus died, He knew full well that I would sin too, yet He died for me anyway—and I believe He would do it again and again in the name of love.

I promise, Jesus knew about you too. He was there when God knit you together, and He knew every way that you would betray Him, just how His disciple Judas did. His love is an invitation into the mess of it all, and it's a promise that you don't have to be defined by it. He lived a life showing us how to walk in holy vulnerability with each other and with Him. I promise, that is where He will meet you.

Let Him wash your feet and receive the gift of love that He freely wants to give to you.

CONVERSATION STARTERS

+ What did you learn about Jesus's character in John 13? It can be something new that you realized or something you were reminded of.

_____

_____

_____

_____

_____

_____

_____

_____

_____

+ Think back on a moment from your past when you experienced the type of love that Jesus modeled when He washed the disciples' feet. Describe it and explain how it felt different from our culture's definition of love.

_____

_____

_____

_____

_____

_____

_____

_____

_____

_____

+ How have you seen a false understanding of love, like Judas's, show up in your own heart?

_____

_____

_____

_____

_____

_____

+ Take a moment to respond and reflect on these questions:
>   + *When is the last time someone experienced Jesus because of the way you loved them?*
>   + *When is the last time you went out of your way to love someone who had nothing to offer you?*
>   + *When was the last time love called you to humble yourself and sacrifice for someone else?*

_____

_____

_____

_____

_____

_____

_____

_____

_____

+ What are some practical ways that you can actively step into Jesus's model of love from John 13?

_____

_____

_____

_____

_____

DELIGHT DATE IDEA

Spend time with your Delight date being real about some of the ways that you've struggled to love people in your life. Discuss some ways that you can hold each other accountable to love deeper and more like Jesus. Think of a specific, practical way that you can show the love of Jesus to your campus and go do it together! It can be as simple as buying someone's coffee or going out of your way to send a couple of encouraging texts to people who might need it.

MY DELIGHT DATE'S NAME: _____

DATE/TIME/PLACE: _____
_____

HOW I CAN BE PRAYING FOR MY DELIGHT DATE:
_____
_____
_____
_____

OTHER NOTES: _____
_____
_____
_____
_____
_____
_____
_____
_____
_____

"a new
command
I give you...
as I have
LOVED YOU
so you must
LOVE ONE
ANOTHER."

john 13:34

WHEN YOU'RE READY TO BE FULLY ALIVE

John 14-15

Last week we left the disciples in an intense moment in the upper room with Jesus. We're picking things back up this week in John 14, still leaned in and listening intently to the final words of Jesus in that intimate room in Jerusalem the night before the Passover celebration.

Before we jump in, I want you to put yourself in the shoes of the disciples for a moment. Remember how in John 13 they found out some *craaaazy* news? I can only imagine that they are all feeling pretty *SHOOK*. I mean, can we blame them?!

First, one of them is a traitor.
Second, one of them is going to deny Jesus three times.
Finally, Jesus is leaving them and they can't go with Him.

Talk about too much information to handle! I would be freaking out. But then I remember that Jesus didn't walk with the disciples for three years only to leave them and make them figure it all out on their own. Jesus knew He would be leaving them, and that His Father would send a helper who would eternally be with them and guide them. This was part of the plan all along!

Perhaps that's why John 14 kicks off with Jesus simply saying, "Don't worry or surrender to your fear. For you've believed in God, now trust and believe in me also" (John 14:1 TPT). The Aramaic for this text can be translated to "let not your heart flutter." Jesus was saying, *"Stop freaking out, I got this!"* A few verses later, Jesus answered Philip's inquiry for Jesus to show them the way to the Father. Jesus responded to the disciples:

"I am the way and the truth and the life. No one comes to the Father except through me. If you really know me, you will know my Father as well. From now on, you do know him and have seen him."
John 14:6-7

Jesus gave the disciples a roadmap for oneness with God. *He IS the way, the truth, and the life.* WHOA. Take a second and wrap your mind around the gravity of that statement. Jesus just proclaimed: *"If you want to know My Father; you know Him by knowing Me."* **When we know Jesus, we know God—and knowing God is where our greatest joy, purpose, and life lies.**

We're going to keep building off of these words of Jesus throughout the rest of this week's Scripture. Trust me, there is A LOT packed into this week. Our text is super rich, wildly important, and incredibly pertinent for those of us who are walking in the ways of Jesus today. John 14-16 almost acts as the instruction manual that Jesus left His disciples for when He would no longer be with them in the flesh. That same instruction manual applies to us today.

To be honest, sometimes I get frustrated with my own failed attempts at following Jesus, tempted to throw in the towel and just give up. When my way fails, the next few chapters in John are always the place I go to for encouragement and direction. My prayer is that the next time you're discouraged in your own faith journey, you can fall back on this text as encouragement and direction for how to live fully alive for God. Together we're going to look at four disciplines that Jesus called the disciples to practice in order to stay strong in their relationship with Him. Let's dive into them!

1. Walk with the Spirit (John 14)

Read John 14:1-31.

Imagine the disciples' surprise when in John 14:12, Jesus told them that they would go on to do far greater things than even He did. His work would continue on earth through them, and whatever they asked in His name, He would fulfill. In verse 16, Jesus spoke of the gift that was to come that would make all of this possible.

+ **Who is God sending to be with the disciples? (v. 16-17)**

And I will ask the Father, and he will give you another advocate to help you and be with you forever—the Spirit of truth. The world cannot

accept him, because it neither sees him nor knows
him. But you know him, for he lives with you and will
be in you.

John 14:16-17

We're finally meeting the third party of the Trinity. Father, Son, and Holy Spirit. Jesus told the disciples that they were going to do amazing things in His name, and God would quite literally live inside of them through the Spirit. This Spirit would transform them fully—from the inside out.

The Enduring Word commentary explains that the Greek word used in this text was *parakletos*. It's a rich word that can be difficult to translate in its entirety. It means someone who defends, comforts, and advocates for someone in need. It's often translated to "helper" in modern English, but the complexity of the original word captures the beautiful complexity of the Spirit. The Holy Spirit is so many things: an inner breath or wind that will speak to you and guide you, a powerful Savior who will advocate for you, and an intimate friend who will never leave your side.

The Spirit gave the disciples the strength to do the works of God that they couldn't seem to do on their own. The same is true for us! Have you ever had a moment when you said something encouraging to a friend but you knew it wasn't your own words? Have your feet ever moved to do something before your mind could fully connect? Have you ever known something instinctually that you shouldn't have known by human logic? Those are often signs of the work of the Spirit in you!

But the Advocate, the Holy Spirit, whom the Father
will send in my name, will teach you all things and

will remind you of everything I have said to you.

John 14:26

We stay in close proximity to the Word of God and the heart of Jesus when we actively walk with the Spirit. Praise God that we don't have to do this on our own! The Spirit will do the daily work of reminding us of who Jesus is and what He calls us to do. We simply have to let ourselves be guided by the Holy Spirit living inside of us. When we walk with the Spirit, we walk in the power and authority that will help us carry out God's will and purpose in our lives.

2. Submit to pruning (John 15)

Read John 15:1-3.

In John 14, we found out that God is going to dwell in us through the Spirit. Then in John 15, we're introduced to the idea that God also is going to give life to others through us. We get to actively participate in the works of God!

In this section of our Scripture, Jesus gave His last "I am" statement when He said, "I am the true vine, and my Father is the gardener" (v. 1). If you're anything like me, you probably know absolutely nothing about gardening (I've legitimately killed every plant I've ever owned in a record amount of time). However, in biblical times, the metaphor of a vine and a gardener (or vinedresser) was well-known and understood as a representation of the relationship between the Hebrew people and God.

For example, flip to Jeremiah 2:21 and fill in the blanks on the next page...

I had planted you like a _____ _____
of sound and reliable stock. How then did you turn
against me into a corrupt, _____ _____ ?

SIDE NOTE: *Don't you love some Old Testament sass?! I know I do!*

Although the reference in Jeremiah is negatively referring to Israelites, Jesus spoke new life into this symbolism by saying that He is the vine, His father is the gardener, and His people are the branches. This means Jesus is not separate from us, but is actually a part of us! Our fruitfulness is dependent on our connection to the vine (Jesus). Do you see the switch here? This is MAJOR!

He cuts off every branch in me that bears no fruit, while every branch that does bear fruit he prunes so that it will be even more fruitful.

John 15:2

In verse 2, we're introduced to the idea of pruning from the vinedresser. Pruning, another gardening term, is the cutting away of dead or overgrown branches in order to increase fruitfulness and growth. This sounds like a great thing for plants, but when it comes to our own lives and hearts, this can be a particularly painful process. Cutting away parts of yourself to allow God to breathe new life into you isn't exactly easy.

Some pruning happens gradually as we get older—little changes or tweaks in our character or heart. Other times, pruning looks like an overnight change in circumstances—the cutting away of a relationship, the loss of a dream, or unexpected disappointments or redirections.

In the book *Drawn into the Mystery of Jesus through the Gospel of John*, Jean Vanier writes, "In order to be more present to God, we have to be less present to other things." It's through the letting go of who we've been that we start to understand the clarity of who we are in the hands of Jesus. Our submission to God's pruning of every area of our life ultimately leads us to freedom and a deeper calling in the kingdom of God. It's not always the strongest branches which are used by God, but rather those which are willing to fully submit to the pruning and refining process. It's a difficult decision in the now that leads to living fully alive in the future!

3. Abide/Remain in Him

Read John 15:5-8.

Jesus goes on to give us a deeper understanding of the relationship between the vine and the branches. We're introduced to a new word—*abide*. (Other translations might use *remain* or *stay*.) Jesus says that as we abide in Him, He also abides in us. Let's learn again from Jean Vanier:

To abide or dwell in Jesus is to make our home in him and to let Jesus make his home in us.
We feel at home with him and in him.
It is a place of rest for one another and presence to one another.
— *Drawn into the Mystery of Jesus through the Gospel of John* (pg. 272)

When we learn to abide in the vine, we live in mutual trust, understanding, and reliance upon Jesus. We are always with Him, conversing about what we've already experienced and what's to come. It's a place of friendship and love. It's a place where your heart, mind, and spirit are transformed into the likeness of Jesus. It's a place where the world around you can transform because of the realization of God's love shining through you.

Abiding is about so much more than checking off a daily quiet time, going to church on Sunday, or watching a sermon series online. It's cultivating the place in your heart where you genuinely just want to be with God. It's the process of starting to understand and sense the desires of God for your life. It's the point when it becomes a joy to do whatever the One you love the most asks of you. When we learn to truly abide in Jesus, we become fully alive. Perhaps this is why Jesus is so straightforward when He says this in verse 11: "I have told you this so that my joy may be in you and that your joy may be complete."

4. Live fully alive

Read John 15:9-11.

So, this is the last step in the process: living fully alive!

Jesus wants us to be filled to the brim with joy, fully alive in Him. When we walk with the Spirit, submit to pruning, and abide in Him, then His joy becomes our joy. The ultimate joy of Jesus is to be totally one with His Father, and He wants us to experience that same unity!

Trust me when I say there is no greater joy on this earth than to know that we are loved, seen, heard, and known by God the Father. There is no greater joy than close intimacy to His Son, our Savior. And there is no greater joy than to take the love we've received and in return participate in God's kingdom by loving people abundantly. **The love and guidance that we get from the Father, Son, and Spirit is what leads us to our ultimate joy and the fullness of life.** I love the way that Jesus closes out this portion of

Scripture. He says:

You are my friends if you do what I command. I no longer call you servants, because a servant does not know his master's business. Instead, I have called you friends, for everything that I learned from my Father I have made known to you. You did not choose me, but I chose you and appointed you so that you might go and bear fruit—fruit that will last—and so that whatever you ask in my name the Father will give you.

John 15:15-16

We are invited into a friendship with Jesus! How crazy is that?! Jesus wants to do life with you. Not just Sunday mornings, but *every single* boring, monotonous, mundane day of your life. He wants to do coffee with you in the morning, drive with you to work or school, chat with you on your lunch break, and recap your long day before you fall asleep. He wants your crazy 3:00 a.m. can't-sleep prayers and your tiny silent prayers before a big test or decision. He wants your mountaintop moments and your lowest valleys.

At this moment in John 15, Jesus knew that His physical presence body was going to leave the earth, but His Spirit would continue on with the disciples for eternity. The same Jesus who walked for three years with Peter, Thomas, Andrew, and the other disciples is the *same* Jesus whose Spirit is dwelling inside you. This invitation into friendship with Jesus is available to you. Watch as your life transforms and you experience the fullness of life in unity with the Father, Son, and Spirit of God!

my WHEN YOU'RE READY TO BE FULLY ALIVE story
hayley knowlton

Hi! My name is Hayley, and this is my *"When You're Ready To Be Fully Alive"* story!

This past summer was a summer of numbness, emptiness, and complete desolation for me. I existed in a space of nothingness for months; I felt nothing in my life and nothing in my faith. It felt like wherever I was, I was far away. It seemed like there was a wall between me and everything around me, and no matter how hard I tried, I couldn't break it down. I was sleepwalking with no conceivable way to wake up.

In August, I was ready to just give up. Fighting for joy and fighting for a relationship with Jesus was too hard. I went for a drive one day, and I felt a pull to try one last time before I let go for good. Feeling stupid and doubtful that anything would change, I forced myself to speak to God out loud.

"Please, God, let me feel *literally* anything."

And then the light poured in.

I felt so much in that moment, but the main emotion flooding my heart was joy. The transition from death to life was overwhelming, and I couldn't hold in my laughter or my tears. This was the day I started living *fully* alive.

Jesus proclaimed, "I am the way and the truth and the life."

I had tried to live those empty months without Him, and I honestly felt dead inside. When I opened my heart to Him for just a second, He seized the opportunity and filled me with life. He showed me in that moment that He loved me, He saw me, and He had never abandoned me. I realized then that the half-in, half-out faith I had been leading only brought me anxiety and emptiness. Jesus proved to me that He's the only way, the only truth, and the only life that will fill me.

Abiding in the Lord daily and coming alive in Him, in every season of life, has always been really difficult for me. Going to a secular college, I'm surrounded by distractions that keep me from spending time with Him. When I went back to school the next fall as a completely changed person, I knew I had a lot of work to do. Just like in John 15, I had to let Jesus remove all the parts of me that didn't bear fruit so He could replace them with new parts that would. One by one, the Lord freed me from the temptations that had previously held me captive. Instead of wanting to go out and party, I started craving time with Him. Instead of wanting to meet a boy at a party and receive validation from him, I started looking to the Word for affirmation in who God says I am. Branch after branch, Jesus cut out the desires in my life that only brought me bitterness.

I finally found a home in Jesus, but that doesn't mean I follow Him perfectly. I still find myself wondering if my stressful homework assignment, crush on a boy, or argument with a friend matter to Him. But I've learned that thinking like this minimizes His love for me. The sweetest reality is that He *does* care about all these things, and He wants so badly for us to come to Him with them. God is the most attentive, most loving, and most caring Father. He wants to hear about our days and be an essential part of our daily lives.

After this summer, talking to Him and spending time in the Word has shifted from being a chore to being a place where I can *come alive*. At the end of the day when I am exhausted and weighed down, I find rejuvenation in time with Jesus. Of course sometimes I get back to my room and just want to watch Netflix under all my blankets. I try to intentionally remind myself that the only thing that can breathe life into my tired heart is the Lord. This reminder has empowered my prayer life! On my walks to class, in the moments before a hard conversation, or in the hour before I go to sleep, I'm comforted in knowing that the Lord is constantly present.

We cannot have a fully alive relationship with Jesus until we find the fullness of joy within surrender. I couldn't feel this life until I let Him change my heart and shift my priorities. This light is waiting for you. He is waiting for you. He wants all parts of your life, even the parts that seem insignificant. He cares for you unconditionally and will do so forever; He will breathe fullness of life into you when you start drawing near to Him daily. There is no greater source of life than time spent with Jesus. He is here to listen, He is here to guide you, He is here to fill your heart with joy, and He is here to speak truth into your life. He just wants to be with you, solely because He loves you.

Open your heart to Jesus daily. He promises us in John 15:11 that when we abide in Him, He will make our joy COMPLETE! Talk to Him throughout your day, listen to what He has for you, and read about the incredible things He has done. You will begin to crave time with Him more and more, and the ways He will transform your life will amaze you.

CONVERSATION STARTERS

+ What did you learn about Jesus's character in John 14-15? It can be something new that you realized or something you were reminded of.

_____

_____

_____

_____

_____

_____

_____

_____

_____

+ Which of these characteristics best describes how you currently relate to the Holy Spirit? Which characteristic do you want to lean into more?

> + _An inner breath or wind that speaks to you and guides you._
> + _A powerful Savior who advocates for you._
> + _An intimate friend who never leaves your side._

_____

_____

_____

_____

_____

_____

_____

_____

+ Jean Vanier wrote this hard truth: *"In order to be more present to God, we have to be less present to other things."* What is one area of your life that you feel God pruning? How have you resisted?

_____

_____

_____

_____

_____

_____

+ What does abiding with Jesus look like in your day-to-day life?

_____

_____

_____

_____

_____

_____

+ Which step of the process from John 15 do you feel called to grow in the most? Why?
> + *Walk with the spirit*
> + *Submit to pruning*
> + *Abide/Remain in Him*
> + *Live fully alive*

_____

_____

_____

_____

_____

_____

DELIGHT DATE IDEA

Go on an *"abiding"* Delight date this week! Head out into nature, go for a walk or hike, find a new local park, or walk to your favorite spot outdoors. Turn on worship music, soak in the beauty of creation, and talk about the goodness of God in your life with your Delight date. There doesn't have to be any agenda. Simply be with Jesus together!

MY DELIGHT DATE'S NAME: _____

DATE/TIME/PLACE: _____
_____

HOW I CAN BE PRAYING FOR MY DELIGHT DATE:
_____
_____
_____
_____

OTHER NOTES: _____
_____
_____
_____
_____
_____
_____
_____
_____
_____
_____

Jesus answered,
"I am
THE WAY,
THE TRUTH,
AND THE LIFE.
no one comes to
the father except
through me."

john 14:6

WHEN IT IS FINISHED

John 16-19

Let me go ahead and warn you: what we're diving into this week isn't exactly an uplifting, jubilant part of the book of John. We've reached that part in the story when things are about to take a sharp turn for the worse. It's kind of like that point in the last season of your favorite Netflix show, an episode or two before the finale, when it feels like all hope is lost—the battle is looking bleak, the main character is in a coma, the relationship is over, and the tears are flowing.

We've come to a similar moment in the story of Jesus. He is getting ready to be arrested, falsely accused, put on trial, and crucified on a cross. **But Jesus knew the plan all along.**

He knew the plan when He called the disciples to follow Him back in Galilee.
He knew when He turned water into wine in Cana.
He knew when He healed the paralyzed man at the pools of Bethesda on the Sabbath.
He knew when He was writing in the dirt as the Pharisees condemned the woman in adultery.

He knew when He waited before going to Bethany on behalf of His friend Lazarus.

He knew in that sacred moment in the upper room with His closest friends and companions.

Jesus knew He was going to die—under Pilate's captivity—a terribly painful death on a cross, on the hill of Golgotha. As you read though, you'll notice that He didn't rebel or resist, instead He freely gave Himself to death in order to save us all—a true friend, a true teacher, a true Savior.

Take some time and read John 16 and 17 on your own. We're moving quickly through these four chapters of Scripture so I've provided some super brief recaps to help you out.

John 16 overview: Jesus told the disciples that they would face persecution just like He did. But they will also have the hope of the Spirit, who will convict the world of sin and guide them in truth. Their sadness at Jesus's absence would soon turn into joy!

John 17 overview: Jesus closed the conversation with the disciples and prayed to His Father. He prayed for the disciples and for all those who would come to believe in the future (a.k.a. you and me!). He asked that we would be made holy in truth and united in love, experiencing the same unity He had with His Father.

Now that we're caught up, the action begins! In John 18, Jesus and the disciples left the upper room and went to a garden across the Kidron Valley, outside of the walls of Jerusalem. John doesn't mention the name of the garden, but we know it from the other gospel accounts to be the garden of Gethsemane.

SIDE NOTE: *The word Gethsemane means "olive press." Olive presses were used to turn olives into something more valuable: olive oil. The more pressure placed on the olives,* the more oil produced. *The pressing or the suffering of Jesus, although painful, allowed for the outpouring of God's spirit for all. Jesus going to Gethsemane before His arrest is incredibly significant and symbolic.*

Let's read together:

Now Judas, who betrayed him, knew the place, because Jesus had often met there with his disciples. So Judas came to the garden, guiding a detachment of soldiers and some officials from the chief priests and the Pharisees. They were carrying torches, lanterns and weapons.

John 18:2-3

Judas probably was hoping to catch Jesus by surprise and trap Him in a moment of weakness. But Jesus, who knew what was to come, was prepared for this moment. He met Judas and the Roman soldiers at the entrance of the garden.

Jesus, knowing all that was going to happen to him, went out and asked them, "Who is it you want?"

"Jesus of Nazareth," they replied.

"I am he," Jesus said. (And Judas the traitor was standing there with them.) When Jesus said, "I am he," they drew back and fell to the ground.

John 18:4-6

Jesus asked them who they were looking for. They answered, "Jesus of Nazareth." I want you to note that this probably came off more as an insult than a casual greeting. This was the common name that Jesus was called by those who opposed Him. Remember how Philip said nothing good comes from Nazareth before his calling in John 1:46? The same concept applies here—it wasn't exactly glamorous to be connected with Nazareth.

+ How did Jesus respond to His captors? (John 18:5)

Your Bible probably shows that Jesus's response was, "I am he." As *The Enduring Word* commentary by David Guzik explains, the word "he" was added by the translators but is not found in the original text. Jesus actually simply said, "I am." Sound familiar? With those two words, Jesus made the connection to the seven previous "I am" statements He made throughout John. Those two simple words proclaimed that He was in fact the Son of God, the Messiah, and the Savior of the world. It's *such* a powerful statement that as Jesus declared "I am," the entire mob fell backward onto the ground (Marvel movie style)!

In verse 10, we see things *really* get crazy. Out of nowhere, Peter, our passionate disciple, sliced the ear off the high priest's servant, Malchus. Immediately, Jesus told Peter to put his sword away—to let everything play out the way it was supposed to. Jesus knew that He had to suffer in order for glory to come.

After He willingly submitted to the mob, Jesus was taken before several key leaders and ruthlessly questioned by a high priest named Annas and the Roman governor named Pontius Pilate (v. 18-40). Meanwhile, Peter stayed close by.

In the matter of one night, he denied Jesus three times, fulfilling the words that Jesus prophesied earlier in John 13:38.

Go ahead and finish reading the remainder of the story from John 18 all the way to John 19:16 on your own.

We're going to pick back up together in John 19:17 as Jesus carried His own wooden cross from inside the city of Jerusalem all the way to a place called Golgotha or "The Skull" on the outskirts of town. There He was crucified, nailed to the cross He carried, next to two other convicted criminals with one on either side of Him. The soldiers hung a sign above His head that read, "Jesus of Nazareth, the King of the Jews." His mother Mary, Mary Magdalene, and even the writer John stood nearby by as He hung there—taking in His last breaths.

Later, knowing that everything had now been finished, and so that Scripture would be fulfilled, Jesus said, "I am thirsty." A jar of wine vinegar was there, so they soaked a sponge in it, put the sponge on a stalk of the hyssop plant, and lifted it to Jesus' lips. When he had received the drink, Jesus said, "It is finished." With that, he bowed his head and gave up his spirit.

John 19:28-30

Read John 19:17-37.

There on that cross on a hill outside of the city, an incredible supernatural transaction took place. God Himself placed all of the guilt, wrath, shame, and sin that we deserved on the shoulders of His Son. And then with one powerful word EVERYTHING changed. After Jesus drank the wine vinegar, His remarkable life ended with one word in His language—*tetelestai.*

The Greek word *tetelestai* can be translated to "it is finished." But what exactly is finished?

The fulfillment of the prophecies—**finished.**
Jesus's perfect obedience to the Father—**finished.**
The flawed religious system—**finished.**
The power of Satan, sin, shame, guilt, striving, hatred, and death—**finished.**
The mission that God sent Jesus to fulfill—**finished.**

There is something super interesting about the word *tetelestai* that we will only fully understand if we know a little bit about Greek grammar.

GREEK GRAMMAR LESSON

This is very exciting and important so try to stay with me! The word *tetelestai* is not in the simple past tense in Greek, but rather in the perfect tense. Don't know what perfect tense is? Don't worry! I looked it up for both of us! This definition is from the Ezra Project website by Dr. John Bechtle.

Greek Perfect Tense: "The perfect tense in Greek is used to describe a completed action which produced results which are still in effect all the way up to the present."

Basically, the Greek perfect tense describes something that happened in the past and is still happening today. So, when Jesus cried out, "It is finished," He meant, "It was finished in the past, it is still finished in the present, and it will remain finished in the future."

WHOA! The final words of Jesus are the words that our faith and freedom is built on today. They mark the beginning of the life we get in Jesus. His last words are our first words—praise God that we get to live on the other side of "it is finished." With *tetelestai*, Jesus righted our wrongs, erased our debt, and shredded our guilt. Jesus's work of redemption was complete.

Although this truth should give us glorious new life, many of us choose to live like the work of God through the life of Jesus isn't already finished and done. We walk around believing that we still have to fight tooth and nail to defeat all of the sin and shame in our lives. But *tetelestai* means the major battle was won! Because of what Jesus did on the cross, we get to fight our small battles from a place of victory rather than go to war ourselves. **Our victory has already been declared in Jesus!**

Tetelestai doesn't mean that there won't still be challenges ahead. I can guarantee that we are all facing something really heavy in our lives that some days leaves us feeling like we're at war all on our own. But remember that you walk with the power of the Holy Spirit, with King Jesus, on the other side of *tetelestai*. You already know how the story ends—Jesus wins and death loses! Whatever you're facing, hold tight to the truth that Jesus has already won the war for you.

Jesus wins *over anxiety.*
Jesus wins *over depression.*
Jesus wins *over heartbreak.*
Jesus wins *over cancer.*
Jesus wins *over infidelity.*
Jesus wins *over relationship failure.*
Jesus wins *over broken dreams.*
Jesus wins *over sickness and death.*

You live on the other side of *tetelestai*. It is finished! Finish reading the rest of John 19 knowing that hope is on the horizon.

my WHEN IT IS FINISHED story

brittany messer

Hi! My name is Brittany, and this is my *"When It Is Finished"* story.

Reading the story of Jesus dying on the cross brings so many mixed emotions into my heart. One part of me wants to absolutely cry my eyes out, and the other part of me is filled with so much hope because I know how the story ends— Jesus wins!

For as long as I can remember I have struggled with anxiety. It has always been a part of my life in one way or another. In middle school, it bubbled to the surface because duh— middle school. In high school it intensified, so I learned how to cope with it and bury my symptoms. In college, it reached an all-time high during my junior year. I was away from home, flunking one of my classes, heartbroken over a breakup from the year before, and drowning in the never-ending feeling of anxiousness I couldn't shake from my mind.

I remember lying in my tiny twin bed in my on-campus apartment bedroom with the lights off, feeling like my world was crashing and burning. I didn't know how I was going to get all the things done on my never-ending to-do list when all I felt capable of doing was sitting and staring at the wall in front of me. Maybe you've been there too—when the tears won't stop, the next breath feels difficult to take, and your heart feels like it's literally cracking in half.

To be honest, in that moment, I didn't feel like it was *finished*. I didn't feel like Jesus had already declared victory over my shame, sin, and death. I felt like the darkness was winning and I was starting to succumb to it too. Where was Jesus in the midst of my crushing anxiety?

A few months later I found myself at a worship night on campus while I was still battling it out with my anxiety daily. I remember thinking that I really didn't want to go—I had too much to do but my friend convinced me to be there. I sat toward the back of the room, halfway engaged, looking at my phone to check the time, and counting down the seconds until it was over.

Then the band started to play a song I had never heard before. I found myself on my knees by the end of the song with tears streaming down my face again, but not tears from anxiety—these were chain-breaking freedom tears.

There's a peace far beyond all understanding

May it ever set my heart at ease

What anxiety fails to remember is peace is a promise you keep

"Peace" by Hillsong Young & Free

As the song ended, I felt the peace of Jesus wash over me and for the first time I understood the fullness of the final words of Jesus on the cross: *"It is finished."*

His peace in that moment reminded me that at the end of the day, I can always trust that He still WINS over my anxiety. Does it mean that I won't struggle with it? No! Does it mean that I'm broken or unfinished? No! Does it mean that *tetelestai* was Jesus's promise to be with me in the midst of my anxiety? Yes! His peace is always available to me. I simply have to reach out and grab hold of it. That worship night marked the turning point in my battle with anxiety—a battle that I'm still facing today. But I know how this story ends. Jesus wins!

The more that I know my Jesus, spend time with Him, and rest in Him, the looser the grip that my anxiety has on me. It's the moments that I start to distance myself from Him that I notice anxiety rushing back in like an aggressive whitewater rapid. But sitting with my Jesus always leads me back to gentle waters, where the pressure to keep my head afloat dissipates and I get to simply wade in the goodness of God.

Maybe there is some area of your life or world where you've been believing the lie that Jesus is losing the battle. Trust me—He's not! The victory is already His, and because of what He did on the cross, the victory is already yours too! Stop living like you have to fight your own battles and start living like *tetelestai* is actually true. Reach out and let Jesus lead you toward victory, no matter what you're facing. I promise that gentle, healing, restorative waters are ahead with Jesus. It is finished!

CONVERSATION STARTERS

+ What did you learn about Jesus's character in John 16-19? It can be something new that you realized or something you were reminded of.

_____

_____

_____

_____

_____

_____

_____

_____

_____

+ What emotions do you feel when you read about the arrest, trial, and death of Jesus?

_____

_____

_____

_____

_____

+ Think back on a season of "crushing" or "pressing" from your own life. What was something beautiful or valuable that came out of those seasons?

_____

_____

_____

_____

_____

_____

_____

_____

+ In what areas of your life have you been living like "the work of God through the life of Jesus isn't already finished and done?" Why?

_____

_____

_____

_____

_____

_____

_____

_____

_____

_____

_____

_____

+ What would it look like for you to begin fighting your battles from a place of victory rather than fighting for your victory? Share practical steps.

_____

_____

_____

_____

_____

_____

_____

_____

DELIGHT DATE IDEA

Spend some time reading and meditating on John 17 together. Read it together line by line. What parts of Jesus's prayers speak to your heart? How does this prayer challenge you?

MY DELIGHT DATE'S NAME: _____

DATE/TIME/PLACE: _____
_____

HOW I CAN BE PRAYING FOR MY DELIGHT DATE:
_____
_____
_____
_____
_____
_____

OTHER NOTES: _____
_____
_____
_____
_____
_____
_____
_____
_____
_____
_____
_____

whatever
you're facing,
hold tight
to the
truth that
JESUS
has already
WON THE
WAR
for you.

WHEN YOU'RE TEMPTED TO COMPARE

John 20

Look how far we've come! We are getting so close to the end of John—nineteen chapters down and only two to go. Please accept my sincerest apologies for ending last week's reading on such a somber cliff-hanger (so sorry to do that to you!). This week we are jumping straight into some good news: the resurrection! Grab your Bible, open up to John 20, and read verses 1-10.

At first glance, this might appear to be a cute little story about the moment those closest to Jesus found out about the empty tomb. However, I think you'll quickly see how this is actually an extremely relatable (and hilarious) competition between two of the disciples. Let's jump in!

Three days after the crucifixion, Mary Magdalene headed to Jesus's tomb. But when she got there, the stone was rolled away and the tomb was empty.

+ Who did Mary Magdalene go tell about the disappearance of Jesus's body? (v. 2)

She ran to tell Peter and the "disciple that Jesus loved." Now, let me remind you of the identity of this beloved disciple: it's John, the author of this gospel, talking in third person about himself (…LOL).

SIDE NOTE: *A lot of commentaries note the humility of John because he chose not to name himself in his writing. I personally would beg to differ. I'm not sure "humble" is the word I'd use to describe referring to yourself in third person as the "disciple that Jesus loved."*

After Mary ran to tell John and Peter about the empty grave, both men immediately set out for the tomb. Obviously they were in a hurry to get there because they had just heard the crazy, life-changing news that the tomb was empty. But I think there was perhaps one other factor driving their speediness. Read the next few verses and take count of the number of times that John tells us that he outran Peter.

So Peter and the other disciple started for the tomb. Both were running, but the other disciple outran Peter and reached the tomb first. He bent over and looked in at the strips of linen lying there but did not go in. Then Simon Peter came along behind him and went straight into the tomb. He saw the strips of linen lying there, as well as the cloth that had been wrapped around Jesus' head. The cloth was still

*lying in its place, separate from the linen. Finally
the other disciple, who had reached the tomb first,
also went inside. He saw and believed. (They still
did not understand from Scripture that Jesus had to
rise from the dead.) Then the disciples went back to
where they were staying.*

John 20:3-10

1. "The other disciple outran Peter and reached the tomb
first" (v. 4)
2. "Then Simon Peter came along behind him" (v. 6)
3. "Finally the other disciple, who had reached the tomb
first" (v. 8)

**This is hilarious. Not once, but three times, John points
out that he beat Peter in a foot race.**

The tomb was empty! Christ was risen! And in the midst
of this world-changing news, John low-key made sure that
everybody would know who had run faster. I'm not sure
I've ever related to anything more. This story reminds me
of the *humanity* of the disciples. They were just like you
and me—**more distracted by competition and comparison
than the gravity of the empty tomb.**

But the John versus Peter rivalry didn't stop there!

We're going to break the rules a little bit and do something
we haven't done yet by skipping ahead to next week's
Scripture. In John 21, we see this continued theme of John
and Peter's competition, plus how Jesus responds to it.

FAST FORWARD
A few days after Jesus was resurrected, the disciples were
back in Galilee, out fishing. (You'll learn more detail about

this story next week.) They hadn't caught any fish and were about to give up when a man (Jesus) walked up on the shore and told them to throw the nets to the other side of the boat.

He said, "Throw your net on the right side of the boat and you will find some." When they did, they were unable to haul the net in because of the large number of fish.

Then the disciple whom Jesus loved said to Peter, "It is the Lord!" As soon as Simon Peter heard him say, "It is the Lord," he wrapped his outer garment around him (for he had taken it off) and jumped into the water.

John 21:6-7

Are you starting to notice the rivalry in this Scripture? John wrote that he reached the tomb before Peter. He was the *first* to believe in the resurrection (John 20:8) and he also noted that he was the *first* to recognize Jesus on the shore. (*That's three points for John!*) But while John was the first to recognize Jesus, Peter was the most passionate in his devotion. So much so that he jumped into the water and swam to Jesus, conveniently leaving the hard work of bringing in the net to John and the other disciples.

Once Peter arrived on shore, he had a very powerful encounter with Jesus. We'll dig into it more next week, but to summarize, Jesus addressed Peter's three denials (John 18) and commissioned Him forward:

Jesus said, "Feed my sheep. Very truly I tell you,
when you were younger you dressed yourself and
went where you wanted; but when you are old you
will stretch out your hands, and someone else will
dress you and lead you where you do not want to
go." Jesus said this to indicate the kind of death by
which Peter would glorify God. Then he said to him,
"Follow me!"

John 21:17b-19

In verse 18, Jesus spoke of the difficult future and calling that lay ahead of Peter. Peter was to die a martyr for the message of Jesus. I can't imagine he was thrilled with this news, but check out verse 20 for his initial response and concern.

+ Who did he ask Jesus about? (v. 20)

You read that right: it's his good pal John! Peter was more focused on John's calling and relationship with Jesus than his own. Instead of keeping his eyes locked on Jesus and boldly saying yes to what He was asking Peter to do, he looked to the people around him.

Peter asked, "Lord, what about him?" Whew. Are you feeling personally attacked right now or is it just me?

How many times have you looked at the people around you and asked God, *but what about them?* I find myself wondering why I can't have more of what other people have on the daily. Questions like this ring through my mind:

Why does she have a boyfriend and I don't? Why does she get so many opportunities? But what about my dreams and passions? Why is she so perfect?

Comparison even seeps into my walk with the Lord. The brutally honest truth of my own heart is that I feel confident that I know the voice of God until I notice someone else who seems to hear His voice better.

Peter's moment with Jesus reminds me of the ugly truth that **comparison will always kill contentment**. Think about it. How many times have you been content with what you have until you see someone else who appears to have it better?

We scroll through Instagram for five seconds and suddenly start hating our bodies. We feel confident in our abilities until someone else comes along with more experience. We are proud of our accomplishments until we hear about the girl who is 5 years younger and 10 times further along in her career.

Comparison is a nasty merry-go-round that most of us can't seem to escape, but I love how Jesus responds to Peter's moment of comparison. I think it speaks so much to what Jesus would say to our comparison games if He was sitting face-to-face with us today.

Jesus answered, "If I want him to remain alive until I return, what is that to you? You must follow me."
John 21:22

In other words, He said: *"Peter, your only assignment is*

to follow Me. Don't worry about him. Stop looking to the people around you to define yourself. You do what I called you to do."

I one thousand percent believe that Jesus is speaking the same thing over our comparison struggles. I imagine the conversation going a little bit like this...

Us: *But why does she have a boyfriend and I don't?*
Jesus: *What is that to you? Follow Me!*

Us: *But why does she get so many opportunities?*
Jesus: *What is that to you? Follow Me!*

Us: *But what about my dreams and passions? Am I not good enough?*
Jesus: *What is that to you? Follow Me!*

Us: *Why is she so perfect? Why didn't You make me more like her?*
Jesus: *What is that to you? Follow Me!*

I imagine Jesus sweetly saying to all of us: *"Stop looking at her...look at Me!"*

The truth is, you can't wholeheartedly follow Jesus while comparing yourself to the person next to you. If your heart is too busy comparing, I'm afraid you will miss the very thing that Jesus has set apart for you to do.

Hard truth time: You will never be that girl you see on Instagram or up on stage.

...AND PRAISE GOD FOR THAT!

God doesn't need two of her. He needs her... and He needs YOU! He has perfectly and uniquely created you and given you the gifts and capabilities to do precisely what He has set out for you. **Don't let comparison steal your story and your calling!** Quit trying to be her or be better than her and simply sink into who you know Jesus made you to be.

Peter momentarily let comparison distract him from his Father, but Jesus reminded him that true contentment would only come through Him. The same is true for you and for me—lasting satisfaction will only come through a real relationship with Jesus. It's through the confidence in that relationship that we are able to take daily steps of obedience, listening to His voice sweetly reminding us to simply follow Him!

We've all fallen victim to comparison and we probably all will again in ten minutes, but next time you find yourself wishing your life was different, wanting more of what someone else has, or making sure that you measure up to the girl next to you—stop for a moment and hear the voice of your loving Jesus speaking truth, kindness, and encouragement about who you are and what He created you to do.

Don't let comparison steal your story.

my WHEN YOU'RE TEMPTED TO COMPARE story

sarah pagnanelli

Hi! My name is Sarah, and this is my *"When You're Tempted To Compare"* story.

For as long as I can remember, I've struggled with comparison. I've compared the way I look, my grades, my gifts, my talents, and even my relationship status— or *lack thereof*. See, I'm 21 and have never been in a real relationship. Yep, I said it. That picture perfect (or maybe cringeworthy) first kiss story? Can't relate.

While I have been lovingly reminded over and over again of God's willingness to provide a future love story well worth the wait, my lack of dating history often affects the way I see myself. I mean there has to be *some* reason for my seemingly never-ending single status…right?

Am I not pretty enough? Not cool enough? Not good enough?

There have been so many moments when I've been awkwardly included in a conversation with a group of girls while they talk about their boyfriends, hookups, and breakups. Society assumes that I would have at least something to add to the conversation, but I'm always ashamed to admit that I really have nothing to give.

But this comparison trap doesn't just stop there. Comparison has slipped into other parts of my life without me even realizing it. About a year ago, I stepped into a ministry leadership role on my campus with a group of my friends. At the beginning of each school year, there is a national leadership conference where women from all over the country come together for a few days of worship, community, and training.

This past August, my team and I decided to attend together. I vividly remember walking into the conference venue with my fellow leaders. At first, I was wide-eyed and excited to meet and learn from so many awesome women, but it didn't take long for comparison to stop me in my tracks.

As soon as I walked through the doors, it started...*My outfit wasn't cute enough. I couldn't speak or pray like the other girls. My story wasn't good enough. It wasn't anywhere close to as powerful as the girl next to me, and on top of that, I didn't have nearly enough wisdom to share advice with the girls around me or on my campus.* The lies of comparison reverberated throughout my mind for two whole days.

On the last night of the conference during worship I finally felt like I was connecting with God—until I opened my eyes to see so many girls on their hands and knees in prayer. *C'mon God, why aren't You bringing me to tears like that?* These girls clearly seemed to hear His voice in a much better and clearer way. My moment with God came to a screeching halt.

I had truly convinced myself that these girls were the perfectly imperfect Christians I so desperately wanted to be (but had no shot at ever being). Just like Peter's moment with Jesus, there I was in a moment of worship, so close to encountering the Lord, but still letting comparison steal the show! I sometimes wonder what I would've experienced if I had kept my eyes locked on God in that moment of worship instead of the women around me.

How often have I looked at the gifts, characteristics, and stories of the women around me, and wished I had more of what they had? As I've continued on in my leadership journey, there have been countless times I was flooded with doubts and an overwhelming sense of defeat. *I didn't say the right thing, didn't pray the right prayer, didn't prepare enough, etc. How could anyone possibly learn anything from me? I am so not qualified.*

It has been extremely difficult to find a place of comfort and contentment in all of this. But I love what Jesus said to Peter in John 21:22, "What is that to you? You must follow me."

I don't know about you, but that verse takes so much pressure off of my shoulders! How freeing it is to realize that Jesus wants me—and He wants ALL of me. My lack-of-relationship, sub-par-outfit, stumbles-over-her-words, complete-and-full self.

Even better news? He also wants YOU and all the fill-in-the-blank stuff you bring to the table.

When I think about my story and experiences, I often wish that I hadn't let comparison steal so much from me. Just like Peter, it is still easy to let those thoughts distract me from God. But I can just picture Him stealing the pen right out of comparison's hand, saying, *"You don't get to write her story, I do."*

My hope is that you allow yourself enough grace to let your eyes fall from the scoreboard. To fully comprehend that you are loved, beautiful, and unique. That your individual value cannot be replaced. When jealousy and comparison threaten to take over, remember Jesus's blunt but freeing words to Peter. God has given you what you need to live out your best life and your calling. Let's rejoice in that today and every day!

CONVERSATION STARTERS

+ What did you learn about Jesus's character in John 20? It can be something new that you realized or something you were reminded of.

_____

_____

_____

_____

_____

_____

_____

_____

_____

+ We saw in John 20 how Peter and John competed with one another. Who in your life are you tempted to compete with or compare yourself to? Why?

_____

_____

_____

_____

_____

_____

_____

+ What is the area of your life that takes your gaze off of Jesus and fixes it onto comparison the most? (Body image, schoolwork, career goals, your faith journey, etc.)

_____

_____

_____

_____

_____

_____

_____

_____

_____

+ How can you let these challenging words of Jesus on
comparison ring true in your life: "What is that to you?
Follow me!"? Think of one practical way that you can stop
letting comparison steal your story.

_____

_____

_____

_____

_____

_____

_____

_____

+ This might feel weird to say out loud, but what is
something uniquely beautiful about you that you haven't
been fully embracing because of comparison?

_____

_____

_____

_____

_____

_____

_____

_____

DELIGHT DATE IDEA

Comparison begins to lose power in our life when we call it out for what it is. Make a list of the places in your life where comparison has slipped in. Go back and forth with your Delight date sharing ways that you've both personally struggled with comparison and look for similarities. Spend time praying through each of these areas and talking about a tangible way that you can begin to celebrate that area of your life rather than compare it to others.

MY DELIGHT DATE'S NAME: _____

DATE/TIME/PLACE: _____
_____

HOW I CAN BE PRAYING FOR MY DELIGHT DATE:
_____
_____
_____
_____
_____
_____

OTHER NOTES: _____
_____
_____
_____
_____
_____
_____

COMPARISON
will always kill
CONTENTMENT.

WHEN YOU'VE MESSED THINGS UP

John 21

Here we are! We've reached the end of John and it's our last week together. What a journey it has been! I love that we're getting to end things together this way. John 21 is my absolute favorite chapter in the Bible. There is so much packed into these 24 short verses *(cue the sigh of relief that you only have to read 24 verses this week!)*.

This moment in John is so powerful to me because I fully believe that there is going to come a moment for each of us when following Jesus gets hard—when we're tired, when we've messed up, and perhaps when we're ready to quit.

But the good news is that in those moments, we're not alone. Some of God's most devoted followers struggled so deeply with failure that they almost lost sight of the calling that Jesus had so clearly spoken over their lives. One of those people is this guy we've gotten to know pretty well over the last few weeks: Peter. We're going to meet him in a desperate moment in John 21. I believe this will help us see how God is calling us to respond when we fall short of the purpose He's spoken over our lives.

We're going to pick up where we left off last week. Remember at the end of verse 20, Jesus appeared several times to the disciples. First, on the night of His resurrection at the gathering of the disciples. Then, eight days later when doubting Thomas put his hands in the side of Jesus to feel His wounds. Now we're about to witness the third reappearance of Jesus to His disciples at the Sea of Galilee.

We're not sure how many days later this encounter took place, but some way and somehow, a group of the disciples including Peter and beloved John have made their way back to their homes in Galilee. Let's catch up with them…

Afterward Jesus appeared again to his disciples, by the Sea of Galilee. It happened this way: Simon Peter, Thomas (also known as Didymus), Nathanael from Cana in Galilee, the sons of Zebedee, and two other disciples were together. "I'm going out to fish," Simon Peter told them, and they said, "We'll go with you." So they went out and got into the boat, but that night they caught nothing.

John 21:1-3

Peter suggested going fishing. We're not entirely sure what Peter was thinking here, but to me it seems as though he was almost saying to the other disciples, *"Hey, let's go back to what we know how to do. Let's get life back under control. I know we did all this cool stuff with Jesus over the last couple of years, but life was a lot simpler when we were just fishermen."*

Let's not forget that a few days or weeks earlier, Peter denied Jesus not once but three times. I can't imagine the shame, self-doubt, and discouragement he was probably dealing with internally. Peter probably didn't feel "enough" for the calling Jesus placed on his life. At the very least, he probably wanted to forget everything that had just happened and numb the pain with something familiar.

We might not be tempted to go fishing when we're upset (I know I'm not), but in moments like this, it's a lot easier to turn on Netflix to numb the pain than to come face-to-face with our failures. I'm not sure I blame Peter's decision to fish because I'd be discouraged, too. I think I'd be pretty upset that things didn't turn out the way I thought they would.

Think about this: for three years, the disciples walked with the headliner. They were in the spotlight. Their expectation was not that Jesus would go to the cross, but that He was going to overthrow the Roman Empire and save the Jewish people. They thought He was going to sit on the throne of David and take back Jerusalem once and for all. But Jesus had announced that sort of thinking was wrong. The Kingdom would come someday, but in order for that to happen He had to go to the cross, and they were all going to suffer.

This was not the outcome the disciples expected.

Jesus went to the cross, and they were left with three dark days of turmoil and mourning. Then they heard the magical words: "He's risen!" Can you imagine how their hearts leapt with joy? *He's alive! He's coming back! Here we go again! The dream is alive again!*

But Jesus didn't show up immediately—and when He finally made an appearance, He showed up in some weird ways. The disciples were gathered in a room, and there He was (John 20:19). He showed them the wounds, ate with them, and then left again (John 20:24-29). Don't you think you'd be a little discouraged at this point too? No wonder they gave up and went back to what they'd always known.

When Peter brought up the idea of returning to their nets, the rest of the disciples all agreed. So, they went out and got into the boat. They fished all night, and they didn't catch a thing. Each time they pulled in their net, it was empty.

Early in the morning, Jesus stood on the shore, but the disciples did not realize that it was Jesus. He called out to them, "Friends, haven't you any fish?" "No," they answered. He said, "Throw your net on the right side of the boat and you will find some." When they did, they were unable to haul the net in because of the large number of fish."

John 21:4-6

The text says that after an unsuccessful expedition the day broke, and a man appeared on the beach. At first, the disciples didn't know it was Jesus.

The guy on the shore called out: *Hey! How's it going out there?*

They replied: *It's terrible! We fished all night and caught nothing!*

The guy on the beach actually told them to try something new—to throw their net on the other side of the boat. When they pulled the net back in, it was *full of fish*. John tells us that Peter put his robe on, climbed overboard, and sloshed or swam through the water to meet Jesus while the others rowed the boat ashore.

Now we all know that Peter had a flair for the dramatic but this feels a tad extreme. Why would Peter jump off the side of the boat and swim to meet Jesus? Maybe because this isn't the first time this miracle has happened.

FLASHBACK TIME
Pause and flip to Luke 5. Read verses 1-11. (This is a more in-depth look at the story at the calling of Peter as a disciple that's summarized in John 1.)

Isn't it ironic that the same miracle—catching all those fish—happened when Peter was originally called as a disciple? Peter and his friends couldn't catch a thing until Jesus appeared and asked if He could use their boat so the crowd listening to Him could hear Him better. They agreed, and rowed offshore a little bit with Jesus in the boat. He finished His teaching and the crowd dispersed.

He then turned to the fishermen and asked, *"How's fishing going?"*

They replied, *"It's terrible! We fished all night and caught nothing."*

Jesus responded, *"Row out a little further and put your nets in again."*

When they did, the net was so full of fish that it began to break with the weight of them. Jesus turned to Peter and spoke an incredible calling over his life: *"Peter, get up. Follow Me. From now on you will no longer be just a fisherman, but you will become a fisher of men."*

Whoa! Pretty surreal! Okay—flashback over. Let's return to John 21.

Peter jumped off the boat and swam to Jesus. I can't help but think that Jesus planned this second miracle to remind Peter of when he was first called to become a disciple, so he would remember that moment when Jesus was so compellingly real, so totally worthy of Peter's life, that he'd give up anything and leave everything behind for Jesus and for His mission.

For us, in those moments when we're discouraged because life isn't turning out the way we thought it would, Jesus empowers us to go back to the moment of our callings. You see, there will be moments in your life when it feels easier to go back to your old way of life than to keep moving forward for Jesus, but God is sweetly calling you to remind your heart of that day when Jesus was so compelling, worthy, and real. Reflect on the point at which you knew, without a doubt, that you would give it all for Him. Ask yourself: *What has changed? Has Jesus changed? Have the needs of people changed? Has the mission changed? Or have I changed?*

Go back. Remember that day. Remember your calling. (You can also re-read Week 1 for more on this!)

As Peter ran to the shore and the other disciples joined him, the text says something super interesting. If you don't look closely, you might even miss it.

And when they got to shore, they noticed a charcoal fire with some roasted fish and bread.
John 21:9 TPT

+ What kind of fire was burning? (v. 9)

John only had so many words to tell this story, so we can trust that every detail is important. Why does he say they found a charcoal fire that Jesus had lit? It's more significant than just describing the type of fire; the Greek word for "charcoal" is only used twice in the New Testament—in this text and in John 18 when Peter warmed himself in the courts before and after denying the Lord.

Now because it was cold, the soldiers and guards made a charcoal fire and were standing around it to keep warm. So Peter huddled there with them around the fire.

John 18:18 TPT

+ What kind of fire did Peter stand by to keep warm?

Yep! *Charcoal.* You know how certain aromas bring back memories? I can't help but wonder, as Peter ran to the shore, if the aroma of the charcoal didn't immediately remind him of the aroma of the charcoal fire where he had betrayed His Savior and friend.

As they sat and ate breakfast together, Jesus addressed Peter's failure around that fire and said, *"I know that you failed, but Peter, I still desperately want to use you."*

Go ahead and read John 21:15-19.

At this charcoal fire on the shore, Jesus called Peter back. He asked Peter a similar question three times, mirroring the three denials from the week before—causing Peter to come face-to-face with his failure. But this time, every time Peter said yes, Jesus responded with "feed My sheep."

He essentially said, *"Peter, I know you denied Me, I know you failed, and I know you might want to choose the easier path. But I need to know if you love Me or not. Because if you love Me, the calling stays the same: **feed My sheep.**"*

Don't you love that? **Our failure has no ownership over our calling.**

Jesus can actually be *glorified* through our failures! He doesn't need you and me to always be at our best. He doesn't need our perfection. He doesn't need us to be spectacular and larger than life. So many of us are under the impression that God is most visibly present in us when we get it all right, but this conversation between Peter and Jesus reminds us of the profound truth. Jesus is still present in us when we don't live up to our own grandiose expectations of what it means to follow Him.

Peter probably wanted to say to Jesus, *"I messed it all up! I turned my back on You. There's no way that You can use my life anymore."*

But Jesus said, *"Hey Peter, do you love Me?"*

Feed My sheep.

I can imagine Jesus looking at Peter and saying in the most compassionate yet convicting way: *"I know you're tired, I know this isn't easy, I know you feel unequipped, but I just need to know if you love Me or not. Because if you love Me, the calling stays the same!"*

Feed My sheep.

Maybe you're reading this right now thinking to yourself: *I'm not cut out for this Jesus thing. I've messed up too much. If you only knew the condition of my heart. If you only knew the things I've done in my past.*

I think Jesus is asking you one question: *"Hey _____ , (insert your name) do you love Me?"*

Feed My sheep.

Or maybe you're reading this thinking: *I'm too busy to love others well, to disciple women, or to be used by God. I need to focus on my grades and other things.*

"Hey _____ , (insert your name) do you love Me?"

Feed My sheep.

Jesus, I can't do this anymore, this calling means dealing with people that I can't stand and that I don't support and believe in. These relationships are too hard....

"Hey _____ , (insert your name) do you love Me?"

Feed My sheep.

Jesus, I haven't spent time with You. My heart wants other things more than You. I just can't get it right no matter how hard I try!

"Hey _____ , (insert your name) do you love Me?"

Feed My sheep.

Our usefulness in the kingdom of God isn't teetering on our successes or failures. If you love Jesus, He can (and will) use you! Your failure doesn't take you out of the game. Your mistakes don't take you out of the game. Your imperfection doesn't take you out of the game. **Your denial of Jesus won't even take you out of the game.**

All that matters is your love for Him. Do you love Him? Do you really love Him? Do you love Him enough to stay true to the mission when things get tough? When He feels distant? When things don't go your way? When you're called to sacrifice? When the glamour and the sparks fade?

Jesus knew what was to come for Peter and how *agape* love would be the only thing that could prepare him for future hardships. In verses 18 and 19, Jesus spoke also of Peter's death—when he would be crucified on a cross just like his Savior. (Man, talk about hardships to come!)

"Very truly I tell you, when you were younger you dressed yourself and went where you wanted; but when you are old you will stretch out your hands, and someone else will dress you and lead you where you do not want to go." Jesus said this to indicate the kind of death by which Peter would glorify God. Then he said to him, "Follow me!"

John 21:18-19

Peter went on to lead the beginning of the Jesus movement and in the end, his last days on earth were marked by total surrender to Jesus and His mission despite Peter's past denials and failures. Doesn't that give you so much hope for how Jesus might use you and your story?!

I fully believe that you are not reading this study by accident. You didn't join the Delight community by accident. You did not end up reading through John with us by accident. God is going to use your life in extraordinary ways, even though at times it might be hard to remember why Jesus is worth it. Satan is going to use anything that he possibly can to try and tempt you away from your mission. He will use your past, your comforts, and your failures to convince you that it's just too hard or that you're just not enough for this calling.

But it's in those moments that you have to go back and remember the sweet aroma of what God has done in your life—the chains of sin that broke during moments of worship, the freedom you experienced through prayer, the declarations you made within Christ-centered community. Those moments are your reminder of the calling that Jesus has placed on your life, that He is bigger than the situation you're currently facing, and that your surrender and love for Him is so much more important than your success and perfection. Can't you hear Jesus sweetly whispering to you?

Do you love Me? **Feed My sheep.**

Do you believe I am bigger than your failures, shortcomings, and mistakes? **Feed My sheep.**

Do you really love Me? **Feed My sheep.**

Your failure has no claim on your future.
Your fear has no claim on your future.
Your mess-ups have no claim on your future.
Your doubt has no claim on your future.
Your feelings have no claim on your future.
The enemy has no claim on your future.

Jesus says simply, *"Follow Me."*

In Him you will find freedom and purpose for what lies ahead.

my WHEN YOU'VE MESSED THINGS UP story

justine groenink

Hi! My name is Justine, and this is my *"When You've Messed Things up"* story!

Any time that I've read John 18 in the past, I've struggled to understand how Peter could do what he did. It seemed impossible to me—how could he turn his back on his friend, the Son of God and his Savior? It wasn't until this past summer, when I found myself in my own Peter moment, that I finally understood. Let's backtrack for a minute so I can give you a glimpse into what my walk with God looked like up until this moment.

I was raised in the church—I attended Sunday school, Bible classes, youth group, the works. My loving parents sent me to a small Christian school where my life became a bubble full of Scripture, doctrine, and tight-knit community. The summer after high school, I decided it was the perfect time to make my faith my own. I ventured off to Mexico for a mission trip, made a profession of faith at church, and joined a local Bible study. I had always felt God's presence in my life, never doubting for a second what I believed.

In some ways, I resonated so well with Peter, who was personally trained by Jesus and brought up in the faith. I never doubted my walk with the Lord and couldn't fathom ever walking away from Him or doubting His goodness. However, when my faith was tested, I easily fell into the same sin Peter did—denial, shame, and doubt.

In June of this year, my pastor took his own life. It was out of the blue; I never imagined it would happen. We had grown super close over the past year, and it broke my heart to see him go. I'd never had such a close friendship with a pastor before. He was young, only 34, and he always seemed to ask me how I was really doing, not just casually wondering like, "I'm good, how are you?"

I didn't know how to cope with his absence. Much like Peter, I lost my spiritual mentor. Losing this person with whom I was so closely connected, and who was deeply involved in my relationship with God, totally put my faith on the rocks. I was like a ship lost at sea, not knowing where to look for guidance. I questioned everything I had learned from him, and whenever I looked to the Lord for support, I was only reminded of the sharp pain of the grief I was experiencing.

My pastor's funeral took place a week after his death, and just one week after that I was flying off to the Dominican Republic for a medical mission trip. Despite everything that had happened, I was honestly excited to get away from it all and dig deep in God's Word during the two-week trip. I had struggled to come to terms with my pastor's death but felt like I was on the right track toward getting over it all, as I progressed through the different stages of grief. (*What a lie I had been feeding myself!*)

I had all these expectations of what I wanted out of this mission trip, like spreading God's Word to those who hadn't heard it, strengthening my relationship with the heavenly Father, and feeling the Holy Spirit's presence. Instead, I couldn't even open my Bible. I couldn't talk to God—*not a single word.* There were so many emotions and I felt them all. I doubted God's presence, His purpose for my life, and why He had to call home the one person in my life that gave me assurance in what I believed.

Instead of running to God with all of my problems, like I had done so many times before, I ran away from Him. Just like Peter went fishing after the death of Jesus, I so desperately wanted to run to something that would numb my pain, taking me away from a face-to-face confrontation with God where I'd have to deal with everything I felt.

That's when I heard Him calling me. *"Justine, do you love Me?"*

It wasn't God who had shut the door on me—I had shut the door on Him. He beckoned me back into His loving arms. He showed me an unimaginable grace, waiting for me to stop running from all of my fears and to realize that I truly did need Him.

Jesus's question to me was so simple, yet so powerful. What simple words of encouragement, that even in my mess-ups, God was still searching for my heart and striving to use me for His glory! My denial, much like Peter's, was not the breaking point of my relationship with Jesus. I absolutely love that John 21 ends with a vision for Peter's future. **God plans to have us move beyond our failures and feelings of defeat to something greater—being a light in the darkness and glorifying His name.**

I was finally able to experience freedom from my denial and shame during a Christian conference this past August. The leaders gave us time to share with a small group about what we were wrestling with at that moment, and what was holding us back from fully committing ourselves to God. That night, I poured my heart out to the girls at my table, telling them all about my struggles and lack of communication with God. In that moment, after facing my fear—realizing that I *did* love God, and wanting to continue a relationship with Him—I was able to see my future more clearly. I could tell that God had something bigger for me, beyond what I was currently facing. I now know that God pulled me out of my denial to glorify Him, whether that means spreading my story of His grace to the women in my Delight chapter or just coming alongside girls in my community who need encouragement through their own times of denial.

When God asks, *"Do you love Me?"* He is giving you the opportunity to embrace freedom from what is holding you back from experiencing Him more fully. Saying yes allows you to break the chains of denial, shame, and doubt. You can clearly hear God calling you back to His presence with those four little words. If you do love Him, your calling hasn't changed—nothing can hold you back from the future God has in store for you.

CONVERSATION STARTERS

+ What did you learn about Jesus's character in John 21? It can be something new that you realized or something you were reminded of.

_____
_____
_____
_____
_____
_____
_____
_____
_____

+ Like Peter with fishing, when you face shame, disappointment, or discouragement in your walk with Jesus, what are you tempted to go back to for comfort?

_____
_____
_____
_____
_____
_____
_____

+ Identify something from your past that you have been letting define your future.

_____
_____
_____

_____

_____

_____

_____

_____

_____

_____

+ Take some time to reflect back on a moment from your life when Jesus was so compelling, worthy, and real. Like the aroma of the charcoal fire to Peter, what can you do to remind yourself or go back to that moment in your heart?

_____

_____

_____

_____

_____

_____

_____

_____

+ Jesus had a purpose for Peter despite his failures. What do you feel Jesus leading you to step into in this next season of life?

_____

_____

_____

_____

_____

_____

_____

_____

DELIGHT DATE IDEA

For your final Delight date of this series, go back and visit page 11 when you reflected on who you knew Jesus to be before diving into the book of John. Talk with your Delight date about some of the things that you've learned and how you've grown closer to Him since then. Answer these questions together:

+ *What was your favorite week?*
+ *What is your biggest takeaway?*
+ *How do you want to keep growing in your relationship with Him?*

MY DELIGHT DATE'S NAME: _____

DATE/TIME/PLACE: _____
_____

HOW I CAN BE PRAYING FOR MY DELIGHT DATE:
_____
_____
_____
_____
_____
_____

OTHER NOTES: _____
_____
_____
_____
_____
_____

your **FAILURE** has no ownership over your **CALLING.**

WHO IS JESUS TO YOU?
the after...

We've reached the end of our journey through the book of John together! Spend some time reflecting on what you've learned about Jesus over the last ten weeks. Just write what comes into your mind. What do you know about Jesus today? How have you experienced Him? How is He more real to you today than He was ten weeks ago? How do you want to continue getting to know Him?

_____

_____

_____

_____

_____

_____

_____

_____

_____

_____

_____

_____

_____

_____

_____

_____

_____

_____

_____

_____

_____

THANK YOU TO OUR AMAZING CONTRIBUTORS!

Sarah Caison

Justine Groenink

Colleen Gill

Margaret Hoyt

Hayley Knowlton

Brittany Messer

Megan Miller

Sarah Pagnanelli

Jordan Smith

Makayla White

MacKenzie Wilson

RESOURCES

The Enduring Word Bible Commentary from David Guzik
"Bible Commentary." Enduring Word, January 14, 2019. https://enduringword.com/bible-commentary/.

The Gospel According to John by D.A. Carson
Carson, Donald Arthur. *The Gospel According to John.* Grand Rapids: William B. Eerdmans Publishing Company, 2016.

The Ezra Project
"The Ezra Project." Ezra Project. Accessed November 22, 2019. https://www.ezraproject.com/about.

Drawn into The Mystery of Jesus through the Gospel of John by Jean Vanier
Vanier, Jean. *Drawn into the Mystery of Jesus through the Gospel of John.* London: Darton, Longman and Todd, 2004.

John for Everyone by N.T. Wright
Wright, N. T. *John for Everyone.* London: SPCK, 2004.

Icons from page 16 and 17
Icon made by [feepik] from www.flaticon.com

start a
DELIGHT

HELP US SPREAD THE WORD ABOUT DELIGHT!

There are thousands of college women all across the country that need Christ-centered community but have no idea Delight exists! We need women like you to help spread the word.

If this community has impacted your life in any way, don't you want to help other women experience it too?

If you know a friend who loves Jesus and who would make an amazing Delight leader–tell her about Delight! With just a few texts you could indirectly reach hundreds of college women on another campus!

How cool is that?!

www.delightministries.com

Point them to our website where they can sign up to bring Delight to their campus! Once they sign up, they will hear from us and will get everything they need to make this community happen at their university.

So... send a couple texts, call a couple friends, maybe post about it on your socials, and let's reach a million more college women together!

For more information, resources, or
encouragement head to...

WWW.DELIGHTMINISTRIES.COM